THE REUNION

THE REUNION

by Peter Gordon

JOSEF WEINBERGER PLAYS

LONDON

THE REUNION
First published in 2010
by Josef Weinberger Ltd
12-14 Mortimer Street
London W1T 3JJ
www.josef-weinberger.com
general.info@jwmail.co.uk

ISBN   978 0 85676 335 9

Printed by Good News Press, Ongar, Essex

To all the friends I have known, and
those I have yet to meet.

CHARACTERS

JENNY

NIGEL

KAY

THOMO

MALCOLM

LORRAINE

MUGSY

SHIRLEY

The action takes place in the function room of a Public House somewhere in Yorkshire. The time is the present.

ACT ONE

A function room in a Public House somewhere in Yorkshire. The general decor of the room is fairly plain and functional. It is well used and rather seedy. Up centre is a small platform on which is set a gaudily painted wooden cabinet which apparently conceals a disco console. The cabinet is painted amateurishly with the words "Rockin Eddie's Mega Disco". Left of the platform is a door which leads onto a corridor. A trestle table is positioned up stage right. A white cloth, concealing a buffet, is draped over the table. Three "pub type" tables with accompanying chairs are positioned down left, down right and up left. Centre stage, down from the platform, is a clear area forming a small dance floor.

As the curtain rises, JENNY, *in her thirties, is arranging the cloth over the buffet. She glances guiltily over her shoulder before turning back to the table and picking up a sausage roll. As she takes a bite from it,* NIGEL *and* KAY *enter.* NIGEL *is in his early forties and well dressed in slacks, collar, tie and jacket. He has a slight northern accent.* KAY *is equally well dressed but her accent is strongly home counties rather than northern.*

NIGEL   Ah, here we are . . . here we are.

                  (JENNY, *hearing his voice, tries to chew the
                  sausage roll as quickly as possible. She keeps
                  the remainder of it concealed in her right
                  hand.* NIGEL *stares around the room, reliving
                  memories.*)

                  God it takes me back. Twenty five years.

                  (*He glances round to see that* KAY *is totally
                  ignoring him, looking around the room with
                  distaste.* JENNY, *meanwhile, is still struggling
                  with the sausage roll in her mouth, obviously
                  having discovered something slightly
                  unpleasant in it.*)

Twenty five years, Kay, since I stood here in this room . . . on this very spot. (*With great satisfaction and finality.*) Here we are.

KAY   Very nice, darling . . . lovely.

NIGEL   Changed a bit mind but, nevertheless (*Looking towards* JENNY *and coughing politely.*) . . . well, here we are.

(JENNY *turns to face* NIGEL, *struggling to speak.*)

JENNY   (*trying to smile pleasantly*) Harro.

NIGEL   Nigel Winter . . . booked the room. Assume everything's in order . . . paid deposit by Mastercard . . . gold card actually . . . yes?

JENNY   Yeah, ethpecting you.

NIGEL   And my wife.

JENNY   Harro.

KAY   It's Kay, actually.

NIGEL   That's right . . . Kay. Kay Winter.

JENNY   Harro.

KAY   Hallo.

NIGEL   Good. Formalities over. Don't suppose any of my party have turned up yet. Always were a bit unreliable . . . on the time front . . . still.

JENNY   Sor . . . af seen anyborr . . . (*With a final grimace and huge effort to swallow the sausage roll.*) Sorry, 'aven't seen anybody.

NIGEL   (*glancing at his watch*) Ah well, still early doors eh? Early doors. We've just driven up from Cambridge. I used to live around here of course, in the area . . . long time ago.

JENNY   Right. I were just finishing laying out your buffet.

NIGEL   Good . . . fine . . . (*Suddenly concerned.*) . . . our what?

JENNY   Buffet.

NIGEL   Buffet? I didn't order a buffet.

JENNY   You did say Winter?

NIGEL   I certainly did. Winter by name but sunny by nature as my friends say . . . their little joke.

JENNY   Well, it were definitely Winter. Bloke rang up a couple of days ago . . . said he wanted 'buffet laid on. Another one of your party mebbe.

NIGEL   (*mystified*) Yes . . . perhaps. Bit out of order though. They could have let me know . . . *should* have let me know in fact.

JENNY   Anniversary is it? We get a lot o' those.

NIGEL   No, no. Reunion actually . . . old mates . . . old muckers.

JENNY   Right. Well I'll just talk yer through your selection then. Five-fifty per 'ead finger buffet . . . that's you yeah? VAT included.

NIGEL   Well, I don't know.

JENNY   (*confidentially*) If you pay cash we may be able to sort your VAT. Let me know before I write out t' bill. All right, luv? Right, I'll talk yer through it.

NIGEL   Ah, good. Kay?

KAY   Yes, darling?

NIGEL   Come and inspect the buffet, Kay . . . please.
                 Rather more your department than mine.

KAY   (*sitting at the table down left*) I've seen a
                 finger buffet before, Nigel.

NIGEL   Yes, but you haven't seen this one. (KAY
                 remains seated.) Ah, good . . . splendid.
                 (*Moving towards* JENNY.)

JENNY   (*lifting the front of the cloth up*) Finger buffet
                 for fourteen, right? Right . . . there's your pork
                 pie, your pickled onions and your gherkins . . .

NIGEL   Good . . .

JENNY   Your cheese and onion quiche and your side
                 salad with your lettuce, cucumber and radish
                 and your fancy frilly cut tomato . . .

NIGEL   Excellent . . .

JENNY   You only get straight cut tomato with your
                 four-fifty spread.

NIGEL   Right . . . absolutely . . . I can see you would.

JENNY   Then up that end there's your mushroom vol-
                 au-vents, mini savoury crackers, crisps, and
                 cheese and pineapple chunks . . .

NIGEL   Marvellous.

JENNY   And your selection of freshly made sandwiches
                 . . . 'am, egg and cress, beef and cottage cheese
                 in your baps and your sliced . . . crusts
                 removed with your five-fifty per 'ead.

NIGEL   Right . . . very nice touch that. Very stylish.

JENNY   And finally your selection of iced fancies and
               your rum and sherry trifle. If you'd gone for the
               four-fifty it'd just 'ave been sherry.

NIGEL   Good . . . good. You've done us proud.

JENNY   Coffee laid on at the end with your individually
               foil wrapped complimentary mint chocolate.

NIGEL   Tremendous.

JENNY   Oh . . . (*With uncertainty.*) and there's your
               sausage rolls . . . forgot to mention your
               sausage rolls.

NIGEL   Oh, right. Splendid . . . fine. Sausage rolls.
               What buffet would be complete without eh?
               Thank you very much. (*Uncertain what else to
               say, he offers his right hand.*) Congratulations.

               (JENNY *quickly transfers the remains of the
               sausage roll to her left hand before shaking
               hands with him.*)

JENNY   We like to think we lay on a good spread.

NIGEL   Absolutely. Well done . . . very well done
               indeed.

               (NIGEL *glances down suspiciously at his right
               hand as they break away.*)

JENNY   Right then, I'll get on. I'll come and 'elp serve
               up your trifle and coffee when you're ready.
               You know where t' bar is for your drinks?

NIGEL   Oh yes . . . yes we do.

JENNY   (*moving towards the door*) 'Ope you enjoy
               your evening.

NIGEL   Yes . . . sure we will. I'm sure we'll enjoy this
               lot . . . brilliant. Fit for a king. Veritable feast!

(JENNY *exits.* NIGEL *examines his right hand more closely, brushing it with his other hand. He finally wipes both his hands on the white cloth and peers suspiciously at the buffet.*)

(*glancing over to* KAY) Doesn't seem much here for five-fifty per head!

(NIGEL *starts counting things on the plates.*)

KAY   I'm just pleased, Nigel, that it's only a buffet. I'd hate her to have to talk us through a six course banquet!

NIGEL   Even so . . . still. Thing is . . . who ordered it! Still, the sandwiches seem up to standard. Very nice beef by the looks.

KAY   Now, darling, you won't forget our pact I hope.

NIGEL   What pact?

KAY   No red meat, Nigel. Very bad for the cholesterol.

NIGEL   Right. No red meat. (*Eyeing the sandwiches again.*) I'm sure the odd one wouldn't harm. They do look rather . . . you know.

KAY   Fine, darling. If you want to have beef, you have beef. Just don't come running to me when all your arteries have furred up. All I'm saying is that we had a pact.

NIGEL   But it's easier for you . . . what with you being a vegetarian. (*Counting again.*) Thing is . . . why are there only twenty-seven sausage rolls! They've made a mistake here . . . there're only twenty-seven sausage rolls. Make a note, darling . . . I'll have a word later. (*Moving towards* KAY.) So, what do you think then?

KAY   What am I supposed to think? It's a back room . . . in a public house.

NIGEL   Ah, but, the thing is, it's more than just a floor, ceiling and four walls. This is a box that contains memories of my youth. This room used to be my second home.

KAY   (*screwing her face up*) It certainly has your Mother's sense of decor.

NIGEL   Course, it's changed a lot since my day.

KAY   For better or worse!

NIGEL   Well . . . different. It was a games room then . . . darts, bar billiards, that sort of thing. The nights I've spent in here. Happy days, I can tell you.

KAY   I dread to think. So, are you going to get me a drink? I can see this being a very long and very trying evening. I don't know why I let you talk me into coming with you. I don't know why you want me here. What's my function?

NIGEL   Function? Well you don't have a function. No point changing the status quo, darling. You're simply here so that you can meet everyone! See my roots.

KAY   Yes, well your roots are already showing.

NIGEL   (*fingering his hair nervously*) They're what?

KAY   No, Nigel, not your 'Just for Men'. We've only been up here an hour and you're all "mates and muckers". I thought you'd grown out of that.

NIGEL   Ah . . . well.

KAY   (*glancing around the room with distaste*) All right, Nigel, for your sake I'll try . . . I suspect I'll have to try very hard, but I'll try.

NIGEL	Well done. Thank you, my sweet. It'll be all right . . . trust me.
KAY	Trust you? That's exactly what you said when you persuaded me to go on that ridiculous holiday last year.
NIGEL	(*sheepish*) Yes, well, not my fault . . . accidents happen. I mean . . . even the Titanic sank!
KAY	The Titanic wasn't on the Shropshire Union Canal!

(MUGSY *enters. He is about the same age as* NIGEL *and speaks with the most broad northern accent of all the characters. His movements tend to be rather slow and lumbering, as is his mental agility. He is, however, a hugely enthusiastic character. One of his pet words is 'magic' and every time he uses it he gives an enthusiastic thumbs-up sign with both hands. He is dressed in jeans and t-shirt, his jeans hanging several inches too low. He carries several electrical leads in his hand. As he enters he moves towards the disco equipment.*)

MUGSY	(*cheerfully*) 'Ow do.
NIGEL	(*glancing over his shoulder*) 'Ow do . . .

(KAY *gives* NIGEL *a withering glance and he realises that his accent is slipping again.*)

	(*quickly*) How do . . . How do you do.
MUGSY	Great. I'm yer disco.
NIGEL	Splendid (*Suddenly realizing what was said.*) Our what!
MUGSY	Yer disco.

NIGEL

I'm sorry but this is getting ridiculous! (*Turning to face* MUGSY.) A buffet is one thing but we definitely didn't order . . . (*In astonishment.*) Bloody 'ell!

(MUGSY *looks back at* NIGEL. *For a moment there is silence as* MUGSY'S *mental powers work overtime.*)

MUGSY

Bloody 'ell! Bloody 'ell!

NIGEL

Mugsy! (*To* KAY *in mixed surprise and trepidation.*) It's Mugsy!

(MUGSY *rushes down from the platform and grabs* NIGEL'S *hand in a vice-like grip. He stares at* NIGEL *in amazement.*)

MUGSY

(*lost for any other words*) Bloody 'ell!

NIGEL

(*half smiling*) Well . . . bloody hell.

MUGSY

Don't tell me, don't tell me . . . it'll come, it'll come. Skegger . . . no, no . . . not Skegger. It'll come, it'll come. I've got yer . . . I've got yer . . . Bazza . . . bloody 'ell, it's Bazza! (*Grabbing* NIGEL *in a bear hug.*) Bloody 'ell . . . you've changed a bit.

NIGEL

(*gasping for breath*) No . . . no.

MUGSY

You 'ave. You bloody 'ave.

(MUGSY *finally releases* NIGEL.)

NIGEL

It's not Bazza . . . I'm not Bazza.

MUGSY

You what?

NIGEL

It's Nigel . . . (*Quickly.*) Nige. (*Glancing quickly at* KAY *who disapproves of "Nige".*) Nigel.

MUGSY

Nige? Nige! Not you! Frosie . . . Frosie Winter?

NIGEL   (*embarrassed at his nickname*) Well, yes, but
             nobody calls me that now.

MUGSY   Well . . . bloody 'ell.

NIGEL   Absolutely . . . bloody hell indeed. (*To* KAY.)
             Look, Kay, it's Mugsy.

KAY   (*pleasantly*) Bloody 'ell.

NIGEL   What? Ah, yes, very good . . . very humorous.

KAY   Now that we've all stopped swearing at each
             other would you care to introduce me properly?

NIGEL   What? Oh, yes . . . Mugsy, this is Kay, my
             wife. Kay, Mugsy.

MUGSY   (*grabbing* KAY'S *hand and pumping it
             furiously*) 'Ow do, Kay. It's right good to meet
             you.

KAY   Mutual, I'm sure.

MUGSY   Aye. (*Stepping back and looking* NIGEL *up
             and down.*) Well, bloody 'ell. What brings you
             to this neck o' t' woods?

NIGEL   Ah . . . knew you'd ask . . . thing is . . . reunion.

MUGSY   Yeah? Great . . . magic.

NIGEL   Yes.

MUGSY   What of?

NIGEL   Well . . . you know.

MUGSY   Oh, right . . . yeah. Yeah. (*Thinking deeply.*) I
             don't think I'm with you.

NIGEL   No? Right . . . (*Taking the plunge.*) Well, you
          know . . . you'll remember . . . how a load of us
          used to go around together . . . meet up in here.

MUGSY   Yeah . . . yeah.

NIGEL   Well that last night . . . when we all met up . . .
          we were all going our separate ways weren't
          we?

MUGSY   I were going in t' army.

NIGEL   That's right . . . you in the army, me to
          University. Don't you remember . . . we made a
          pact, a sacred vow, to meet up twenty-five
          years on, to the very day. No matter where we
          were . . . what we were doing, we said we'd
          make every effort to get back and meet up in
          here.

MUGSY   Did we? Right . . . yeah. (*Thinking deeply.*) I
          don't think I remember that.

NIGEL   Well, hardly surprising. I should think you
          were probably unconscious.

MUGSY   Oh, right. You don't think anybody'll remember
          d' you?

NIGEL   Well, I wouldn't worry . . . you were usually
          unconscious by the end of the night . . .
          weren't we all!

MUGSY   No, about meeting up again. It's a long time,
          twenty-five year.

NIGEL   Well, obviously I wouldn't just leave it to
          chance, would I? That's why I sent out
          reminders. I traced everyone and sent them an
          invitation.

MUGSY   Oh right. Right, great, magic. You were always
          dead organised you. (*Suddenly puzzled.*) You
          didn't send me one.

NIGEL   Well, no, no I didn't. Couldn't trace you. But
               you're here . . . that's the main thing . . . you're
               here.

MUGSY   Bloody 'ell, I am aren't I? I'm yer disco you
               know?

NIGEL   Ah . . . point of order. I don't think we
               requested a disco. There's only going to be
               seven of us . . . plus partners . . . fourteen
               maximum. Fifteen with you . . . if you're
               staying.

MUGSY   That dun't matter. Your disco's automatic. If
               you book t' function room you get me free. It's
               dead lucky that isn't it?

NIGEL   (*uncertain*) Well, lucky . . . yes . . . that's one
               perspective. Thing is, with only a small number
               of us it's hardly worth the wear on your stylus
               is it?

MUGSY   No, it's all right 'cos I 'ave CDs and digital as
               well . . . they don't wear.

NIGEL   Ah . . . that's reassuring.

MUGSY   Yeah. Eh . . . magic eh?

NIGEL   Brilliant.

MUGSY   I'll finish setting up then. Just a few leads 'ere
               and there. Bloody 'ell . . . it'll be magic. Blast
               from the past eh? Magic. (*Moving to the
               platform then turning back for a parting shot.*)
               Bloody 'ell!

               (MUGSY *climbs onto the platform and fiddles
               about with leads as* NIGEL *sits down next to*
               KAY, *a resigned look on his face.*)

NIGEL   Oh dear . . . oh dear, oh dear, oh dear.

KAY	What?
NIGEL	Worst nightmare. He wasn't meant to be here. I didn't invite him.
KAY	Why not? He seems harmless enough.
NIGEL	Well, he is . . . in his own way. It's just that he was never really one of us. He always kind of hung on. Whenever we went anywhere there was always Mugsy. You couldn't even chat up a girl without turning round and finding Mugsy breathing down you neck. (*Doing an impersonation of* MUGSY.) Eh . . . bloody 'ell, magic eh?
KAY	I think he's rather sweet.
NIGEL	Thing is, he rather lacks it . . . (*Tapping his head.*) up here . . . you know.
KAY	But it's not as though he wants to perform brain surgery on you, or anything like that. The poor man only wants to play you a song.
NIGEL	Well, that's another thing isn't it! His taste in music. He used to like Adam and the Ants! He's like a leach, you can't get rid of him. The first time . . . the very first time I ever took a girl to the pictures, Mugsy turned up and sat in between us eating popcorn.
KAY	And who was this, Nigel . . . your very first date?
NIGEL	Oh, huge mass of dark hair . . . very spotty. Can't remember her name. I bet she remembers Mugsy though. He walked home with us. Talk about romantic first date . . . me, her and Mugsy with a bag of chips and mushy peas. Reeking of vinegar.

MUGSY	Right . . . we're there. Magic. 'Ey, I've got a good one for you. Blast from the past . . . see if you remember this one eh?

(MUGSY *fiddles around trying to find a record.* NIGEL *looks highly depressed.*)

NIGEL	Oh dear . . . oh dear, oh dear.

MUGSY	(*finding the right record*) 'Ere we go, guys an' gals, rave from the grave.

(*As* MUGSY *puts the record on, a commotion is heard from the corridor off.*)

THOMO	(*off*) S'all right, love, I know the way. I've been here a time or two I can tell you. (*Singing the opening of "Walk of Life" as he approaches the doorway.*) "Daa-da. Da-da-da-da-da-daa-da. Da-da-daa-da. Da-da-da-da-da-daa-da. Whoo-hoo".

(NIGEL *and* MUGSY *both raise their heads, listening.*)

MUGSY	Bloody 'ell . . . it's Thomo! Magic.

(THOMO *appears in the doorway. He is dressed in slacks and an open necked shirt with a large chain and medallion round his neck. He pauses in the doorway for effect.*)

THOMO	(*shouting*) Come on then, Frosie . . . get the bloody drinks in!

(*He pulls himself up to his full height and with his shoulders back gives a curious little twitch of the head which he believes to be authoritative. It is a gesture which he continues to make whenever he is trying to make a point or exert authority.*)

(*An Adam and the Ants song starts to blast out from the disco with* MUGSY *singing and*

*dancing along to it as the lights fade to
darkness. After several bars, the music fades
then rises again in the middle of a different
record. The lights rise. It is a little time later.
Empty and partially full glasses and bottles
are littering the tables.* MUGSY *is still behind
the disco equipment, dancing.* NIGEL *stands
near the buffet table talking to* MALCOLM.
MALCOLM *is very conventionally dressed in
jacket and tie. He wears spectacles, and
always gives the impression of nervousness.*
THOMO *is sitting next to* KAY, *who has a bored
expression.*)

THOMO   (*trying to shout to* KAY *over the music*) So
               Frosie were giving me this lift . . .

KAY   Pardon?

THOMO   I said he were . . . (*Glancing in annoyance at*
               MUGSY.) I said . . .

               (KAY *shakes her head, still unable to hear.*)

               . . . he was giving me this . . . (*Giving up and
               shouting even louder at* MUGSY.) . . . 'ey, give
               it a rest Mugs. 'ey, Mugsy!

               (*He manages to catch* MUGSY'S *eye.* MUGSY
               *simply grins inanely, signalling that he can't
               hear over the music.*)

               (*shouting again*) I know you can't 'ear, you
               pillock. Turn it down will you . . . turn the
               bloody thing off.

               (THOMO *gesticulates at* MUGSY, *who finally
               gets the message and switches the volume off.*)

MUGSY   Dead loud weren't it! Couldn't 'ear you.

THOMO   I couldn't 'ear meself and I was inside me own
               head next to me mouth. Leave it off a bit will
               you . . . give it a rest.

MUGSY   But it's t' disco.

THOMO   Well I know that. I know it is. But we want to
               'ave a natter.

MUGSY   Oh . . . right.

NIGEL   Just for a bit, Mugsy . . . thank you . . . until
               our ear drums stop bleeding.

MUGSY   Oh . . . right. Magic.

               (MUGSY *fiddles about on the platform as the
               others continue their conversations.*)

THOMO   (*to* KAY) He's a daft bugger you know. Two
               more brain cells and he'd qualify to be a
               mangrove swamp. Where was I?

KAY   I really haven't the faintest idea.

THOMO   I know . . . bikes. So Frosty . . . Nige . . . was
               giving me this lift home on the crossbar of his
               bike. Now this Copper peddles past the other
               way and shouts, "No lights". So me, quick as a
               flash, I shouts . . . you'll like this, it'll kill you
               . . . I shouts back quick as anything, "Neither
               'ave we". Eh? "Neither 'ave we". Eh? Good one
               eh? Eh?

KAY   Very good.

THOMO   'Ey, the things we used to get up to. The crazy
               gang, that was us . . . that's what everybody
               called us . . . well, that an' a few other things!

KAY   From what you've told me it appears that none
               of you were ever sober.

THOMO   Sober?

KAY   Correct me if I'm wrong but all your fun seemed
               to emanate from a bottle.

THOMO   Oh no, we were sober sometimes. We must
             have been . . . I'm sure we were. (*Shouting over
             to* NIGEL.) Hey, Frosie, we were sober
             sometimes weren't we?

NIGEL   Sober? Yeah . . . course we were. (*With a rare
             attempt at humour.*) Well, I think we were once.

THOMO   Were once! 'Ey, I like that . . . we were sober
             once. (*Back to* KAY.) 'Ey, sense of humour that
             husband of yours has got. Always had . . .
             'asn't changed. Were sober once, eh? . . . eh?

KAY   Yes, it's his quick wit and repartee that keeps
             us together. Full of one-liners.

THOMO   I know, I know.

             (LORRAINE *appears in the doorway, looking for*
             THOMO. *She is much younger than him,
             attractive and wears a mini-skirt and high
             heels. She is heavily made up.*)

LORRAINE   Thomo . . . Thomo?

THOMO   'Ey, 'ere she is . . . the love of my life. 'Ere you
             are pet . . . get yourself over 'ere.

             (LORRAINE *teeters over to* THOMO'S *side as*
             NIGEL *and* MUGSY *watch in astonishment.*
             MALCOLM *has obviously seen her before.*)

LORRAINE   (*to* MALCOLM *as she moves to* THOMO) Hi, Mal.
             (*To* THOMO.) I were looking for you all over.

THOMO   Well, I was 'ere wasn't I. Lorraine, this is,
             whatsname . . . Kay . . . Frosie's wife. 'E's over
             there.

LORRAINE   'Ave you got me a drink then?

             (LORRAINE *puts her handbag down on the
             table, about to sit.*)

THOMO	No, I 'aven't. Don't you go sitting yourself down either. You can nip to the bar and get us a refill.
LORRAINE	Thomo!
THOMO	It's no use Thomoing me, you should 'ave been here earlier. I'll 'ave a pint and Kay'll 'ave whatever she's on.
KAY	I'm all right thank you.
THOMO	Get away. Wine is it? A white wine for Kay. Get 'em to stick a cherry in it for 'er . . . liven it up a bit.

(LORRAINE *hovers by* THOMO'S *side.*)

Well, go on then! They'll be closing by the time you've staggered there on those stilts.

LORRAINE	I'm waiting for the money!
THOMO	Money! (*Raising his eyes heavenward.*) Tell 'em to put it on t'slate with the food, all right?
LORRAINE	Will they do that?
THOMO	Of course they'll do that. Off you go then. Careful you don't get stuck down any floor boards.
LORRAINE	It's not fair, Thomo. You always make me go for everything!

(LORRAINE *teeters out leaving* THOMO *shaking his head sadly.*)

THOMO	She's all right you know but talk about dim! It's the one thing I've got the wife to thank for. At least while I'm married to 'er it keeps Lorraine off my back.

KAY   Oh, you have got a wife then? I was beginning
           to wonder about that.

THOMO   'Ave I got a wife! Eh? Twenty year . . . give or
           take a lifetime. Very 'ard you know, is marriage
           . . . very limiting. When we tied the knot I
           didn't realise I was tying my 'ands behind my
           back. You didn't think Lorraine . . . ?

KAY   Oh no . . . no, I thought Lorraine must be your
           daughter.

THOMO   Oh . . . right. (*Suddenly realising the
           implication he glances sharply at* KAY *who
           smiles back at him sweetly.*) Right. (*Twitch.*)

MALCOLM   (*to* NIGEL, *confidentially*) Lorraine's not his
           wife you know.

NIGEL   Daughter more like.

MALCOLM   His wife's very nice. Not a bit like him at all.

NIGEL   You've kept in touch with them then?

MALCOLM   I bumped into him a year or so ago. It's more
           him keeping in touch with me really now. When
           he wants an alibi.

NIGEL   Oh, I see . . . right. Very good. So what about
           you then, Mal? Married, divorced, living in . . .
           you know?

MALCOLM   My own house?

NIGEL   No . . . you know . . . sin.

MALCOLM   Oh no, none of those. Go my own way mostly.
           Friends of course . . . a few friends . . . one or
           two.

NIGEL   Good . . . fine . . . excellent. Job?

MALCOLM   Oh, yes. Still at the Co-op down the main
               street, same as ever.

NIGEL   Good . . . good.

MALCOLM   Twenty-seven years come October. Bit of
               excitement a few years back when they moved
               me to the branch on the outskirts, but I'm back
               now.

NIGEL   At the nerve centre . . . good.

MALCOLM   Got on a bit now of course. Assistant to the
               deputy manager.

NIGEL   Right . . . splendid! Getting on, that's the big
               thing. Soon be manager then eh?

MALCOLM   No . . . no, I shouldn't think so. Bit late now for
               manager really. Been passed over a few times.
               Still, I don't think your work's everything is it?
               Best to have time for other interests, you know
               . . . other things.

NIGEL   Oh, absolutely . . . couldn't agree more . . . all
               work and no play. Other things, very important.
               Like?

MALCOLM   Well, this and that, you know. I have a very
               large model railway set up now . . . like I used
               to have, you know . . . but bigger, much bigger
               in fact. Several tunnels now and very extensive
               sidings.

NIGEL   Good.

MALCOLM   For shunting. You wouldn't recognise it.

NIGEL   No . . . no, I don't expect I would. Still . . .
               that's progress eh . . . progress.

MALCOLM   Mother said if I got any more sidings we'd
               probably have to move house to accommodate
               them.

NIGEL   Right.

MALCOLM   We had a good laugh about that.

NIGEL   Good . . . good. How is your Mother?

MALCOLM   Oh, she's still, you know, my Mother. She still
                has the same little problem, you know, with
                her . . .

NIGEL   Right. Still, it's marvellous what they can do
                these days.

MALCOLM   So, what about you?

NIGEL   Oh well . . . married. No children of course. Kay
                would've but . . . terrible financial burden.

MALCOLM   Is she?

NIGEL   No . . . I meant children. Do you know how
                much it costs to raise a child?

MALCOLM   No.

NIGEL   Oh, it's very expensive.

MALCOLM   I expect so.

                (MUGSY *drifts down to join them.*)

NIGEL   As for a job . . . (*Proudly.*) Lecturer. College of
                Further Education.

MALCOLM   Oh, very nice.

NIGEL   Business management, that's me. Moulding the
                minds of the Captains of Industry of the future.
                Head of Department . . . nearly. I should have
                got the job but then someone else put in for it.
                Still, you can't have everything . . . where
                would you put it.

MUGSY   'Ey, did you see Thomo's missus, did you see
         'er eh? Magic.

NIGEL   That's not his wife, Mugsy. I wouldn't go
         spreading it around. Mum's the word, all right?

MUGSY   Oh, right. (*Thinking deeply.*) It's not his first
         Mum 'cos she were definitely older than 'im.
         What do you think to it then eh, what do you
         think, Mal?

MALCOLM What?

MUGSY   Disco. I'm yer disco. That's me that.

MALCOLM Very nice. It's just . . . sorry, but couldn't help
         noticing . . . there's a 'g' in rocking you know.

MUGSY   Oh, aye, I know that. But that's me, Rockin
         Eddie, without a 'g'.

MALCOLM But your name's not Eddie either!

MUGSY   But that's my stage name. Rockin Eddie . . .
         King of Swing. I do bookings. What do you
         think?

MALCOLM Well I wouldn't really know. I don't go to a lot
         of discos.

         (JENNY *enters and moves over to* MUGSY.)

MUGSY   (*sadly*) No, neither do I. (*To* NIGEL.) I've been
         thinking. If you *did* 'ave everything, you
         would 'ave somewhere to put it, 'cos if you 'ad
         everything you'd 'ave the thing you *put* it in as
         well wouldn't you?

NIGEL   What?

MUGSY   What you were saying before. (*Slowly as if
         explaining to idiots.*) If you 'ad everything,
         then you'd . . .

JENNY   Mugs?

MUGSY   Yeah?

JENNY   (*to* NIGEL *and* MALCOLM) 'Scuse me, just a
           quick word with 'im. (*Pulling* MUGSY *to one
           side.*) I think there's summat up wi' those
           sausage rolls.

MUGSY   Why, what's up?

JENNY   Well, I 'ad one. I'm sure there's summat in
           there that shouldn't be.

MUGSY   No, they'll be right. Nowt can go wrong wi' a
           sausage roll . . . I mean, they just sit there,
           don't they.

JENNY   Well I'm telling you, they're dead chewy.
           They're not right. What's happened to yer
           disco?

MUGSY   I'm just 'aving a break . . . taking five. It's a
           reunion. I used to 'ang out wi' this lot. I'm just
           'aving t' crack wi' 'em.

JENNY   Well, I'd take those sausage roll off there if I
           were you . . . if you don't want to poison 'em.

           (JENNY *starts to move away.*)

MUGSY   'Ey.

JENNY   (*stopping*) Yeah?

MUGSY   (*moving to* JENNY) Yer all right, you.

           (MUGSY *gives* JENNY *a kiss on the lips.*)

JENNY   Yer not bad yerself.

           (JENNY *kisses him back, then exits.*)

MUGSY   (*to* NIGEL) She's all right 'er, you know.

NIGEL   No not bad at all, Mugsy. Very, er . . . very
             much your type I would say.

MUGSY   Aye, she's all right. (*Moving over to* THOMO.)
             She's all right 'er.

THOMO   Who's that?

MUGSY   Jenny. She fancies me y'know. She's all right.

THOMO   I'd 'ardly think that's possible, Mugsy . . .
             'ighly unlikely.

MUGSY   You what?

THOMO   Fancying you and being all right. The two
             things are 'ardly of a compatible nature.

MUGSY   (*lost*) Ah . . . right. 'Ey, your old man's done all
             right for 'imself. (*It is* THOMO's *turn to look
             totally lost.* MUGSY *explains slowly.*) Yer
             stepmother . . . she were in 'ere . . . magic.

THOMO   Stepmother! What are you on about, Mugs?
             (*Aside to* KAY.) 'E lives in a bloody world of
             his own. (*To* MUGSY.) I buried my Father two
             year ago, so all in all I reckon 'e's not doing
             that well at all.

MUGSY   You mean 'e's dead!

THOMO   Aye, well they're sticklers round 'ere you know
             . . . the paperwork's a bloody nightmare if you
             want to bury somebody alive! I'm sure they'd
             make an exception in your case though. Yes,
             Mugsy, 'e's dead.

MUGSY   I'm right sorry 'bout that. He were all right,
             your old man. Still, it just goes to show. Maybe
             she were a bit too much for him at 'is age.
             What a way to go though, eh! Bloody 'ell!

(MUGSY *moves back to fiddle with his disco equipment.* THOMO *shakes his head sadly.*)

THOMO   (*to* KAY) He shouldn't be 'ere you know. He was never one of us . . . not one of the elite.

KAY   So I understand.

THOMO   You see, there was eight of us. The magnificent eight. There was us three, then there was Bazza the midget, Skegger . . . Jacko, Fatty Smaithwaite . . . and . . . oh, what's his name? You know . . . thingy.

KAY   I really don't know.

THOMO   I'll know it when I 'ear it. Oh, bloody 'ell . . . it began with a P . . . Pur . . . Prot . . . Pop . . . it'll come . . . it'll come. Maybe it was a T. You'll know it when you 'ear it. Anyway, there was eight of us. Plus Mugsy who doesn't count. In fact, it has to be said, 'e *couldn't* count . . . 'e couldn't do anything much at all. Now, if we're in luck, they'll all be turning up tonight . . . except Jacko of course. Now, 'e killed 'imself on his motorbike just shortly before we all split up . . . it were a nice bike as well. Anyway, 'e won't be coming. The rest of 'em though, they'll be 'ere . . . they wouldn't let us down.

KAY   I really fail to see why you're all doing this.

THOMO   Doing what?

KAY   Meeting up like this. What's the point?

THOMO   What's the point! What's the point? (*Having to think very hard.*) The point is that we promised to . . . we agreed to . . . we're mates.

KAY   How can you possibly be mates with someone that you haven't seen for twenty-five years? You can't even remember all their names! I kept saying to Nigel, I don't know why you're doing this.

THOMO   But we're mates! You must 'ave 'ad mates when you were a young lass.

KAY   But none that I'd want to see after twenty-five years! I've moved on . . . I'm a different person. I admit there'd be a certain satisfaction in seeing what the ravages of time have done to one or two of them, but no more than that.

THOMO   But that's because, and I don't think I'm out of turn in pointing this out, you're a woman, you see, eh? You don't think the same as us. Now, to us . . . our mates are important. We went through all sorts together . . . you never forget . . . see what I'm saying, eh? Oh, what the hell was his name? (*Shouting to* NIGEL.) 'Ey, Frosie, what was his name?

NIGEL   Who?

THOMO   Well if I knew who I wouldn't be asking! You know . . . thingy. (*Moving over to join* NIGEL *and* MALCOLM.) There was us, Fatty, Jacko, Bazza, Skegger and . . . you know 'im, begins with a P.

NIGEL   Stinker.

THOMO   That's 'im. (*Turning to shout to* KAY.) Stinker . . . that was 'im. (*To* NIGEL.) Bloody 'ell, he was a lad wasn't 'e? Do you remember, all the stuff 'e used to nick? No shop was ever safe from 'is thieving little 'ands, eh?

MALCOLM   We have a lot of trouble with that in our shop. We've had to go closed circuit. That's one of my responsibilities actually, to make sure we remember to switch it on.

THOMO   Right. Do you remember that time he dared us
             all to nick a chocolate bar from Sweaty
             Harrison's sweet shop?

NIGEL   (*fondly*) Yeah.

THOMO   And we bloody did it. We didn't let him down.

MALCOLM   I've always felt very guilty about that. All that
             chocolate'll have come out of Mr Harrison's
             pocket.

THOMO   No wonder it was always 'alf melted then, eh?
             Do you get it? 'Alf melted?

MALCOLM   But I can see the other side of it now . . .
             having responsibility in the retail trade. Do you
             know how much money shoplifting costs us per
             annum?

THOMO   Alright, Mal, point made . . . no need to labour
             it son. We only did it for a laugh. 'Ardly the
             worst crime in the world.

NIGEL   And it was twenty-five years ago.

THOMO   Yeah . . . and again last week.

             (NIGEL *and* MALCOLM *both look at him.*)

             Well, I fancied a Mars Bar and I only 'ad
             enough change for my *Daily Sport*. It's all
             right, Malcolm . . . it wasn't the Co-op.

NIGEL   Thing is, Mal, I do share your moral
             reservations, but I don't think you should
             torment yourself. None of us were half as bad
             as Stinker. I blame his parents.

MALCOLM   I don't think they were responsible, were they?

NIGEL   He was the youngest of four though,
             consequently there was always a lot of hiding
             space in his hand-me-down blazers, which is a

great temptation when your that age. I've seen
him come out of WH Smith's looking like Billy
Bunter.

THOMO   What ever 'appened to Stinker anyway?

NIGEL   Last I heard he'd just been made up to Bishop.

THOMO   Bishop! Bloody 'ell, what a waste. I was just
             telling your wife about Jacko.

NIGEL   Jacko? Yeah . . . poor old Jacko.

THOMO   'E'd have gone a long way, I'm telling you.
             Best right foot down our street he 'ad. Bloody
             marvel at free kicks.

NIGEL   Not so good with his left though. In fact it was
             a bit shorter wasn't it . . . his left leg? Don't
             you remember . . . he always had a tendency to
             walk on a bit of a slant.

THOMO   Very good on the side of 'ills though. Tragic
             was that bike accident. They reckon that when
             things like that 'appen, you always remember
             where you were, what you were doing at the
             time. Like when John Lennon was shot.

MALCOLM   I can remember where we were. The three of us.
             We were round at my house. We were trying to
             decide which film we were going to see. My
             Mother came in . . . I can even remember her
             exact words. "Steven's had a motorcycle
             accident . . . he's passed away".

THOMO   Well, she always were one for flowery
             language, your Mother.

MALCOLM   I cried for days. He was my best friend. Of all
             of you . . . he was my best friend. Nothing ever
             seemed quite the same after that.

NIGEL   Yeah . . . well.

(MUGSY *moves down to join them.*)

MUGSY   I can remember where I were.

THOMO   You surprise me. In fact I'm surprised *you* can
         remember where you were five minutes ago.

MUGSY   I were *'ere* five minutes ago!

THOMO   Oh dear . . . you give me a 'eadache you do!

MUGSY   Anyway, like I were saying, I were round at me
         Gran's, 'elping to bath her whippet. It were on
         t' news. Shot they said . . . in New York . . .
         with a gun.

THOMO   (*exasperated*) We're not talking about 'im,
         Mugs. We were on about Jacko.

MUGSY   Jacko? Aye . . . well I can remember that an' all.
         As if it were yesterday. Funny isn't it . . . 'ow
         you remember things like that. You wouldn't
         think that you'd remember things so clearly
         that 'appened so long ago. Aye, I can
         remember.

THOMO   All right, Mugs . . . we've got the gist.

MUGSY   It's like it 'appened yesterday. I can remember
         it dead clear y'know. You never forget summat
         like that.

THOMO   All right, so where were you then?

MUGSY   I were on t' back of 'is bike weren't I? When 'e
         'ad t' crash. It really did me 'ead in did that.
         (*Cheerfully.*) Shall we get t' disco going again
         now then? I've sorted some dead good ones
         out for us.

THOMO   We're talking, Mugs!

         (LORRAINE *teeters back in with a tray with the
         three drinks on.*)

LORRAINE	I've got yer yer drink, Thomo.
THOMO	Right . . . leave it down there. (*Indicating the table where* KAY *is sitting.*)
LORRAINE	Don't you want it now! I wouldn't 'ave bothered if you don't want it!
THOMO	Of course I want it. I'm finishing this one. You sit yourself down and take the weight off your 'eels . . . you'll damage the floor.
LORRAINE	Aren't you coming over to talk to me?
THOMO	I'm busy aren't I . . . talking over 'ere. Talk to Kay.
LORRAINE	But I want to talk to you.
THOMO	What for? Talk to Kay. Tell 'er about your GCSE. (*Turning back to the others.*) Bloody 'ell!

(*The men stand in a circle, talking, as* LORRAINE *sits next to* KAY.)

LORRAINE	'Ello.
KAY	Pleased to meet you.

(LORRAINE *and* KAY *sit in embarrassed silence for several seconds, unable to think of any possible common subject.*)

LORRAINE	I'm with Thomo.
KAY	I'm very happy for you.
LORRAINE	Do you come 'ere often?
KAY	Once will be more than sufficient.
LORRAINE	I'm just 'ere with Thomo.

KAY	Yes . . . I think you mentioned it.
LORRAINE	I got a GCSE last year . . . at night school, you know?
KAY	Very worthwhile.
LORRAINE	Grade E it were. I'm 'oping to get another one sometime. No point rushing it.

(KAY *smiles reassuringly.*)

	I work for Thomo . . . you know. I do 'is typing and 'is books. I'm not so good at typing but Thomo says it doesn't matter.
KAY	Right.
LORRAINE	I'm not so good at t' books either really.
KAY	I'm sure you must have other assets.
LORRAINE	Not really, no. Thomo always says 'e keeps me on for me figure . . . not me figures. He always 'as a bit of a joke with me about it, you know? That's why I took my GCSE . . . just to show 'im really. You with . . . what were 'is name . . . Frosty?
KAY	Nigel. His name's Nigel.
LORRAINE	Oh . . . Nigel. It's a nice name that. I like Nigel. Sort of manly . . . like, Nigel Mansel . . . I've 'eard of 'im . . . I think he used to be a jockey. Yeah, I like Nigel.
KAY	Well, at the moment, I'm not quite sure whether I like Nigel or not.
LORRAINE	Oh . . . right.
KAY	Don't get me wrong . . . I don't mind him coming here to meet with his old friends. It's

just that I knew from the very beginning that I
was going to be a bit of a spare part.

LORRAINE   Oh . . . right.

              (*There is several seconds silence.*)

              Thomo does spare parts . . . with 'is business.
              Spare parts and second 'and cars. He's in the
              motor trade.

KAY   Yes, he rather has the look of someone who
              would be.

              (*There is further silence as the conversation
              passes to the men.*)

THOMO   Aye, I've done all right. (*Handing a business
              card to* NIGEL.) Thompson Motors . . . quality
              cars of distinction from the name you can trust.
              Specialise in the five 'undred to fifteen 'undred
              pound bracket. If you're ever in the market,
              give me a ring. We'll maybe manage you a bit
              o' discount.

NIGEL   Well, very kind but . . .

THOMO   Oh, they're all genuine . . . most of 'em. I'll see
              you right. I fixed Mal up with a tidy little motor
              six months back, top o' the range . . . got it all
              'asn't it, Mal . . . sunroof . . . seats. You're very
              'appy aren't you, Mal?

MALCOLM   (*uncertain*) Oh . . . yes. Well, apart from a few
              little things. I'd like to get it back on the road
              again as soon as possible.

THOMO   Mal . . . you know me. Just as soon as I can get
              you the parts at the right price we'll 'ave you
              mobile again. Leave it with me . . . right? Eh?
              Eh?

MALCOLM   Well, I suppose so.

THOMO

I'd do it under warranty for you, but the warranty unfortunately doesn't cover faults of that nature. Trust me, Mal. 'Ave I ever let you down?

MALCOLM

It's just that these last three months seems to have flown and it's making transport difficult.

THOMO

But the point is, Mal, you live on a bus route don't you? No point paying over the odds for spares when you 'ave a perfectly good integrated public transport system on your door step.

MALCOLM

But the thing is, Thomo, my mother can't manage on the bus.

THOMO

Well get 'er a push bike then! I can't be expected to organise everything for you, Mal! (*Quickly.*) 'Ow about a bit of music for us then, Mugs. Get us in the mood eh?

MALCOLM

But . . .

THOMO

Mal, I won't 'ear another word. Your 'appiness with my service is more than enough reward. Mugsy, go and show him your tweeters and your woofers . . . 'e'll like that.

MUGSY

Oh . . . right . . . magic. (*Putting his arm round* MALCOLM *and leading him on to the platform.*) 'Ey, you can 'ave a look at me records, I've got some right good classics 'ere Mal. You'll remember 'em. Blast from the past.

THOMO

(*twitching, confidentially to* NIGEL) The trouble with Mal is 'e's a worrier. Always was . . . always will be. (*Gesturing to the buffet table.*) You get this lot sorted out. I'll check on the girls, all right?

NIGEL

Ah . . . just one thing.

THOMO

Yes, son?

NIGEL   It's just that . . . well . . . re the buffet . . .
           (*Waving vaguely at the food table.*) . . . are you
           responsible?

THOMO   I didn't make it if that's what you mean.

NIGEL   No . . . order it, I mean did you order it? You
           see, strictly speaking, I was organising this
           reunion and after long and hard thought I
           decided that there definitely shouldn't be food
           . . . food wouldn't be provided.

THOMO   Why not? 'Ave you got an ulcer?

NIGEL   No. Thing is . . . it just didn't seem in keeping
           with our old traditions. We never had food in
           here.

THOMO   Only 'cos they didn't serve it . . . except for the
           pickled eggs. I mean, if you want to penny
           pinch, Frosie, that's up to you but I thought
           we ought to make a bit of a bash of it, that's
           all. No 'arm in that is there, eh?

NIGEL   But *I* was organising. You can only have one
           organiser. That's one of the first principles of
           management. Now, I could have delegated food
           to you but . . .

THOMO   Look, Frosie, if it worries you so much, I'll sort
           the food eh? I'll collect the money and settle
           up, all right? Eh?

NIGEL   (*resigned, starting to take the cloth off the
           food*) Right.

THOMO   I'll 'ave yours off you in a minute then. Eight
           pounds fifty per 'ead it is.

           (THOMO *turns to move towards* LORRAINE. NIGEL
           watches him, open mouthed. SHIRLEY *appears
           in the doorway. She is* THOMO'S *wife and is*

sensibly dressed. THOMO *spots her before she spots him.)*

Oh, bloody 'ell!

(THOMO *darts back behind* NIGEL, *grabbing the cloth from him. He holds it up in front of himself, hiding from* SHIRLEY.)

NIGEL   What are you doing that for?

THOMO   *(whispering)* Nothing. Ignore me. I'm not 'ere.

(SHIRLEY *sees* MALCOLM *and moves to him.)*

LORRAINE   *(to* KAY) Oh 'eck. It's Thomo's wife!

(LORRAINE *shrinks down in her chair, hoping to make herself invisible.)*

SHIRLEY   *(shyly)* Hallo, Malcolm . . . are you all right?

(MALCOLM *tries to point discretely in* THOMO'S *direction.)*

I thought I'd find you here.

(MALCOLM *stabs his finger in* THOMO'S *direction more violently.)*

What? Is there something wrong with your arm? Is it a spasm? Where does it hurt? Shall I give it a massage?

MALCOLM   Thomo's over there. *(By way of explanation to* MUGSY.) Thomo's wife. I expect she's after Thomo.

MUGSY   'Ow do.

(*Shirley, looking concerned, moves down to* THOMO. *As she approaches* THOMO *he peeps out over the top of the sheet and they meet face to face.)*

THOMO   (*in shock*) Aah!

SHIRLEY   Hallo.

THOMO   'Ow do, love. All right?

SHIRLEY   What are you doing here? What are you doing
             with the cloth?

THOMO   What cloth? Oh, aye, this cloth. I were just
             explaining to Frosie 'ere . . . Frosie, the wife . . .
             I were just explaining, wasn't I?

NIGEL   Were you?

THOMO   Aye . . . about the wife's whites. She gets 'em
             to come up far better than this, don't you love?
             It's all in the powder you see . . . and your spin
             whatsname. (*Throwing the sheet casually back
             on to the table. Nervously.*) So, what brings
             you 'ere, love? I thought it was your thingy
             tonight . . . you know, your whatsit.

SHIRLEY   Yoga.

THOMO   Aye, that's it. (*To* NIGEL, *flailing his arms
             imitating yoga positions.*) Gets into all sorts of
             positions she does. The only thing I've seen in
             the same positions as 'er is our cat . . . before it
             'ad its operation that is. (*To* SHIRLEY.) Why are
             you 'ere then, my love?

SHIRLEY   (*hesitant*) I came to see you. You said you'd
             had an invitation to your reunion.

THOMO   But I said I wasn't coming to it. I said I was
             going down the club.

SHIRLEY   Oh, yes. So I'm quite surprised you're here
             really.

THOMO   Right . . . (*Twitch.*) I'm surprised as well,
             you're dead right there. Stroke of luck eh? I'll

get you a drink then. You are stopping are
you?

SHIRLEY   Of course I'm stopping . . . don't you want me
to stop? (*Looking around the room.*) Are these
all your friends? Isn't that Lorraine . . . from
work?

THOMO   Lorraine . . . where? Bloody 'ell, so it is. That's
a turn up isn't it? Fancy 'er being 'ere.
(*Thinking quickly.*) Not entirely unexpected
though . . . now I think about it. She did
mention she was coming along with . . . Mal.
She's 'ere with Mal.

SHIRLEY   Malcolm?

THOMO   I know . . . it's amazing, isn't it. I didn't think
he 'ad it in him. Still, if 'e 'as, I'm sure she'll
get it out of 'im.

SHIRLEY   Mal? Are you sure you mean Mal? She's here
with him?

THOMO   (*joking to* NIGEL, *playing for time*) Am I sure?
Am I sure? Eh, Frosie, am I sure, eh? 'Ave you
met the wife? (*Shouting to* MALCOLM.) Mal, get
yourself down 'ere sharp. (*To* NIGEL.) Frosie
. . . the wife.

            (SHIRLEY *and* NIGEL *exchange polite smiles as*
            MALCOLM *scuttles down from the platform.*)

MALCOLM   (*worried*) Everything all right?

SHIRLEY   I understand that you're here with Lorraine. Is
that right? That can't be right is it?

MALCOLM   Me . . . with Lorraine! No . . . oh no . . . (*As*
THOMO *desperately catches his eye.*) . . . and
yes in a way. Yes and no . . . but mainly yes . . .
probably. (*Looking to* THOMO *in confusion.*)
Definitely yes. Definitely. Definitely yes.

THOMO   I thought so. (*Shouting over to* LORRAINE.) I
               say Lorraine, I say . . . I thought so, eh?

LORRAINE   Mmm?

THOMO   I thought you were 'ere with Mal, eh? Eh, with
               Mal?

LORRAINE   Oh yeah . . . Mal.

THOMO   (*to* MALCOLM) Well go on then, son, don't
               waste your time 'ere.

MALCOLM   What?

THOMO   Get yourself back to 'er. Get stuck in . . . you
               know.

MALCOLM   What?

THOMO   Get stuck in. (*Putting his arm around* MAL *and
               drawing him away from* SHIRLEY.) Make it look
               like you *are* with 'er. Play your cards right an'
               I may 'ave a review of the situation vis-à-vis
               your warranty.

MALCOLM   Oh . . . I see . . . if you like.

               (MALCOLM *ambles away to* LORRAINE'S *side as*
               THOMO *turns back to* SHIRLEY.)

THOMO   Loves young dream eh? I say, loves young
               dream. I've been doing my best at match
               making for weeks. Trouble with Mal is, 'e's still
               got a very immature attitude to the opposite
               sex. 'e's still not worked out why women've
               been put on the same planet as us.

NIGEL   (*smiling to himself at his own perceived
               witticism*) Neither have I as it happens.

THOMO   Neither 'ave I, eh? Neither 'ave I? (*To* SHIRLEY.)
               'Ey, he's a wag is our Frosie . . . 'is one liners!
               Laugh a minute 'e is. 'Ey, Frosie, tell 'er the

one about us being sober sometimes. (*Back to* SHIRLEY.) You see Frosie's wife . . . she said that she thought . . .

(THOMO'S *voice fades as attention turns to* MALCOLM.)

MALCOLM   (*now by* LORRAINE'S *side, shyly*) H . . . hello, Lorraine. H. . . how are you doing?

LORRAINE   I were all right 'til she turned up . . . Thomo won't buy me any drinks now! You're supposed to be wi' me then?

MALCOLM   I believe so. (*Helpfully.*) I could buy you a drink . . . when you're ready . . . if you like.

LORRAINE   Would you?

MALCOLM   Yes. (*To* KAY.) I'm with Lorraine . . . for the evening. (*Panicking.*) Just the evening mind . . . not any longer . . . not, *later*, into the night if you see what I mean. I'll probably buy her a drink though. I'm a bit of an expert on the Co-op's range of wines and spirits. I went on a course.

KAY   Good.

(LORRAINE *glances across and notices* SHIRLEY *watching them suspiciously.*)

LORRAINE   (*to* MALCOLM) Well, if your going to do it, you'd best make it look convincing.

MALCOLM   How do you mean?

LORRAINE   Give us a kiss.

MALCOLM   Oh . . . I don't think so. I'm in the retail trade you know.

LORRAINE   So?

MALCOLM   We have some very good offers on margarine
               at the moment . . . you should call in sometime
               and have a look.

LORRAINE   Oh, come 'ere!

               (LORRAINE *grabs* MALCOLM *round the neck and
               pulls his face down towards her. She kisses
               him.* THOMO *is looking over towards them as he
               still chats to* SHIRLEY *and* NIGEL. *He is
               horrified.*)

KAY   (*to* MALCOLM *and* LORRAINE) Don't let me
               inhibit you in any way.

THOMO   (*to* SHIRLEY *and* NIGEL) Excuse me a moment.

               (LORRAINE *releases* MALCOLM *as* THOMO *walks
               over to them.*)

LORRAINE   (*to* MALCOLM) See . . . that weren't so bad were
               it?

THOMO   What the 'ell are you doing! Eh? Eh?

LORRAINE   I were just trying to make it look convincing
               . . . I thought that's what you'd want.

THOMO   It didn't 'ave to be *that* convincing. (*To*
               MALCOLM.) I 'ope you didn't enjoy that
               (*Twitch.*) . . . I don't want you getting any ideas!

MALCOLM   No I didn't, Thomo . . . not at all. My mind was
               on margarine actually. I think I've priced some
               up wrong.

KAY   (*starting to enjoy herself*) Don't worry, Mister
               Thomo, I think I inhibited them a little.

THOMO   (*scowling*) Aye . . . well I'll inhibit 'em with a
               length o' three by two if it 'appens again.
               Don't forget who you're with young lady . . .
               who's bought your drinks.

LORRAINE	But *I've* bought most of me drinks . . . and most of yours . . . you've been too busy!
THOMO	Aye, well . . . exactly. All right eh? (*To* MALCOLM.) All right? Right, I'm away for another pint. (*Prodding* MAL *in the chest.*) You . . . with me . . . where I can keep my eyes on you.
	(THOMO *straightens himself to his full height and gives his little twitch before exiting with* MALCOLM *in tow.*)
KAY	Such an elegant man!
LORRAINE	You what? Oh yeah . . . Thomo.
	(MUGSY *moves down from his platform to join* NIGEL *and* SHIRLEY.)
MUGSY	(*to* SHIRLEY) 'Ow do. . . right pleased to meet you.
SHIRLEY	(*looking distractedly after* THOMO *and* MALCOLM) Yes, I'm sure.
MUGSY	Right turn up is that eh! Thomo's step mother and Mal! Weird is that.
SHIRLEY	What?
NIGEL	Right. Mugsy . . . you'd better come with me. Bit worried about Thomo and Mal. We don't want any unpleasantness to creep in. This is supposed to be a celebratory occasion.
MUGSY	Magic.
	(NIGEL *strides out followed closely by* MUGSY.)
NIGEL	(*as he passes* KAY) Just off to . . . you know . . . all right my sweet . . . splendid.
MUGSY	(*as he passes* KAY) Magic.

(KAY *gazes heavenward in disbelief. She is suddenly aware of* LORRAINE *watching her.* KAY *smiles at her and* LORRAINE *smiles back. There is silence for several seconds.*)

KAY

Well . . . this is certainly different. I don't think I've had an evening quite like this before.

LORRAINE

Yeah . . . it's nice to 'ave a change isn't it. That's what my Gran used to say . . . a change is as good as . . . something. We had to put her in a home.

KAY

But what is the point of all of this. As far as I can see it's a complete disaster. Nigel would have achieved far more by staying at home and fixing the cistern as I wanted him to do . . . in the en-suite.

LORRAINE

(*tremendously impressed*) Have you got an in-suite!

KAY

En-suite, yes.

LORRAINE

With a bath and everything?

KAY

Shower, low level slim-line wc and bidet . . . all in matching Sorrento Blue with gold fittings . . . fully tiled of course.

LORRAINE

I've always wanted an in-suite . . . I bet it's right luxurious. Just imagine . . . being able to leap out o' bed in the morning and run carefree and naked across your bedroom into your very own shower unit . . . dead glam.

KAY

Yes, well Nigel and I certainly don't go in for that sort of thing.

(SHIRLEY *moves over to join them.*)

SHIRLEY

Hallo, Lorraine.

LORRAINE	(*nervous*) Hallo Missus Thompson . . . how are you?
SHIRLEY	I'm a bit confused really, Lorraine . . . and a bit concerned really.
LORRAINE	Oh.
SHIRLEY	You see I wasn't expecting to find my husband here . . . and yet I do. Then I find him here in the presence of one of his . . . (*Choosing her words very carefully.*) . . . employees.
LORRAINE	Do you? Oh . . . that's me!
SHIRLEY	And then everybody says you're here with Malcolm. I'm a bit surprised about that really . . . and even more confused.
LORRAINE	Oh. This is Kay . . . she's got an in-suite . . . in Sorrento Blue.
SHIRLEY	Hallo, Kay . . . well done.
KAY	Thank you.
LORRAINE	With a bidet.
SHIRLEY	(*embarrassed to ask*) Lorraine . . . did you really come here this evening with Malcolm? Or was that just my husband making it up . . . you know, subterfuge?
LORRAINE	I'm not with you.
SHIRLEY	Perhaps I didn't phrase that very well. Let me put it another way. Are you . . . this is really quite embarrassing . . . are you seeing my husband?
LORRAINE	I see 'im every day . . . I work for 'im!
SHIRLEY	I wouldn't blame *you*, Lorraine. I don't think it would be the first time . . . I shouldn't think it

would be the last either. I'd just like to know
the current situation really.

LORRAINE   I came on me own. Thomo and Mal were
                  already 'ere.

SHIRLEY   But which one are you with?

LORRAINE   I'm just sat 'ere talking to Kay.

KAY   About plumbing. But I can also vouch for the
                  fact that Lorraine arrived alone . . . if that helps
                  at all.

SHIRLEY   I really don't know . . . I just seem to get more
                  and more confused. (*Sitting at the table with
                  them.*) Why can't life be straightforward!

KAY   Because life contains men which immediately
                  turns it into a complete fiasco. Why are we
                  here this evening for instance? What is the
                  point of all of this?

LORRAINE   It's a reunion isn't it . . . Thomo said . . . well,
                  that is, Mal said . . . they both said.

KAY   But why do they *want* to reunite? They can
                  barely remember each others names!

SHIRLEY   My husband *said* that he wasn't coming to it.

KAY   I have a theory. I put it all down to this *male
                  bonding* thing that one hears about.

LORRAINE   What's that?

KAY   Male bonding? Well, it's when otherwise
                  normal, sane men . . . if men could ever be
                  described as normal and sane . . . get afflicted
                  by a sudden urge to rush out and do silly
                  things with other men . . . often involving some
                  sort of chest-beating rivalry. At the end of it,
                  they tell each other what wonderful chaps they

all are and how awful women are for not
understanding them.

LORRAINE   But women have girl friends . . . it's just the
             same isn't it?

KAY   No similarity whatsoever. Women have girl
             friends in order to retain some sense of sanity
             in their lives . . . to talk to about important
             issues. Have you tried talking to men?

LORRAINE   I 'ave a bit of a laugh with 'em sometimes . . .
             you know . . . like, a laugh. (*Aware of* SHIRLEY.)
             Not wi' Thomo of course . . . I don't 'ave any
             laughs wi' 'im.

SHIRLEY   I never have any laughs with him either. He's
             not that sort of person really.

KAY   But the important difference, Lorraine, is that
             women have *friends*, whereas only men have . . .
             (*Forming inverted commas with her finger
             tips.*) . . . mates. With men there's got to be the
             competitive element. Without the competition
             they may be friends but they'll never be mates.

LORRAINE   (*puzzled*) Do you think so? I 'ave mates. We go
             out and get silly sometimes . . . (*Giggling.*) . . .
             it usually involves loads o' drinking.

KAY   But with respect, Lorraine, you are younger
             than us, isn't she Shirley?

SHIRLEY   Yes . . . I suppose so.

KAY   And as a young . . . lady . . . you will grow out
             of that type of behaviour, won't she, Shirley?

SHIRLEY   I expect so yes. She'll become miserable like
             the rest of us.

KAY   (*trying to ignore* SHIRLEY's *last remark*) You
             see, the thing is, Lorraine, that as women
             mature they become more . . . aware . . . more

astute . . . whereas men unfortunately never
improve . . . they are always immature
teenagers. Their skin becomes wrinkled but
their brains remain acned.

LORRAINE   (*taking it all in*) You know an awful lot about
it all don't you?

KAY   Yes, well, it pays to know your enemy. If you
know them you can contain them, which is
what I manage very nicely with Nigel thank you
very much.

LORRAINE   Doesn't he object!

KAY   But that's the secret. The poor dear doesn't
even know.

LORRAINE   You've really got it all worked out 'aven't yer. I
wish I were like you . . . you know, wi' brains
like you. All those ideas *and* an in-suite . . . it
makes you sick really, it does, honest.

            (JENNY *enters and moves towards the table.
            The three of them sit watching her as she
            starts to adjust things slightly on the table.
            She eventually becomes aware of the silence
            and the three pairs of eyes on her back. She
            turns to them.*)

JENNY   All all right? Don't worry 'bout me . . . just
popped in to make sure this were all straight.
You'll be wanting your coffee soon I expect.

KAY   I expect so.

SHIRLEY   Can't wait.

LORRAINE   Lovely.

JENNY   The men seem to be 'aving a whale of a time
through in the bar. I think they'll be fetching
some drinks through for you in a sec.

KAY   I expect so.

SHIRLEY   Can't wait.

LORRAINE   Lovely.

JENNY   Then the evening'll really get going.

KAY   I expect so.

SHIRLEY   Can't wait.

LORRAINE   Lovely.

JENNY   Right . . . everything seems all right.

                  (LORRAINE *waits for her turn in the responses
                  but, after looking at* KAY *and* SHIRLEY *in turn,
                  realises that the others aren't going to speak.*)

LORRAINE   Lovely.

                  (JENNY *moves over to stand near them at the
                  table. She is suddenly a little hesitant.*)

JENNY   Look, I 'ope you don't mind but they said
                  through there that it'd be all right if I joined
                  you. Being sort of with Mugsy who's sort of
                  with your lot . . . your party. Make a nice
                  change from waiting on.

SHIRLEY   No we don't mind. (*Suddenly anxious that she
                  hasn't consulted the others first.*) We don't
                  mind, do we?

KAY   (*bored again*) You're more than welcome to
                  join us. Although I suspect that within five
                  minutes you'll be rushing off trying to find
                  someone to serve somewhere.

JENNY   Oh, I don't think so. Anyway you don't want
                  to be sat around like this. Don't you like to
                  'ave a dance? 'Ere, get yourselves up . . . I'll
                  find summat real good to put on.

KAY   There's really no need to trouble yourself.
               We're quite happy.

JENNY   It's no trouble, honest. All part of the service.

KAY   We wouldn't want to upset Mister Mugsy by
               tampering with his equipment.

JENNY   No . . . he won't mind.

               (JENNY *moves behind the disco equipment and
               searches through records and CDs.* KAY *and*
               SHIRLEY *look less than enthusiastic, but*
               LORRAINE *gets to her feet in the middle of the
               dance floor, ready to join in.*)

LORRAINE   I love dancing . . . it's the only thing I'm any
               good at. Can you find us something dead funky
               . . . I really like that . . . you know . . . dead
               funky.

JENNY   I'm not sure they had *funky* in Mugsy's time.
               Here, try this one. It's one of his latest.

               (*The room reverberates to the beat of a loud,
               fast song.* KAY *and* SHIRLEY *look even more
               glum.*)

               (*shouting at the top of her voice*) Do you like
               this . . . I love this.

               (JENNY *dances her way down to the dance
               floor where* LORRAINE *is also dancing. After
               several bars of dancing,* LORRAINE *dances
               across to the table and shouts at* KAY *and*
               SHIRLEY.)

LORRAINE   Come on . . . join in . . . you'll enjoy it.

               (KAY *looks away in distaste, but* SHIRLEY
               makes the mistake of looking at LORRAINE *and
               shaking her head, embarrassed.*)

               Come on.

(LORRAINE *grabs hold of* SHIRLEY *and pulls her on to the dance floor.* SHIRLEY *has no option other than to join in, but she attempts to dance to it in a very old-fashioned way.* KAY *turns her head to watch them for a few seconds then holds her head in her hands in disbelief. The lights fade as the music quietens. The music gradually fades away as the lights go up to find* NIGEL, THOMO *and* MUGSY *standing with nearly empty plates of food and glasses of drink in their hands. Mal enters carrying a tray with three and a half pints of beer on it. He puts it down on one of the tables.*)

MALCOLM   There's your drinks here.

MUGSY   Magic.

THOMO   Well done, son. Took your time didn't you?

MALCOLM   There was a queue . . . and people kept pushing in.

MUGSY   What do you think to t' sausage rolls, Thomo?

THOMO   Sausage rolls? (*Taking a bite from a sausage roll.*) Aye, very passable . . . very passable indeed.

MUGSY   So you think they're all right, Thomo?

THOMO   (*irritated*) Well, that's what I said isn't it? Very passable. If I'd meant they tasted crap I'd 'ave said, "these taste crap" . . . I wouldn't have said, "very passable"!

MUGSY   Right. I think they taste crap. What do you think Mal?

THOMO   Bloody 'ell! Are we going to spend all night talking about the bloody sausage rolls!

MUGSY   You started it.

THOMO	No I didn't.
MUGSY	Yes you did . . . you said they were very passable.
THOMO	Only after you asked me!
NIGEL	There was one missing, you know. I did an audit of the quantities earlier in the evening and we appeared to be a sausage roll short. Only twenty seven instead of twenty eight. Fourteen into twenty seven doesn't go.
THOMO	'Ardly matters really . . . considering there's only eight of us.
MALCOLM	I don't think eight goes very well into twenty seven either.
THOMO	Does it matter!
NIGEL	Of course it matters. You ordered it . . . I'd have thought you'd be concerned. Thing is, they were supposed to cater for fourteen, and in the sausage roll department they've only catered for thirteen and a half. It's the principle.
MALCOLM	In the retail trade, if a customer asks us to supply twenty eight sausage rolls, and we agree to supply twenty eight sausage rolls, then a verbal contract has been formed.
NIGEL	Exactly. That's what I'm saying isn't it?
MUGSY	Aye . . . but your contract were for a buffet for fourteen . . . the exact number of sausage rolls weren't stipulated.

(*They all look at* MUGSY *in amazement for his logical contribution.*)

THOMO	Careful, Mugs . . . that came dangerously close to rational argument!

NIGEL   But the fact remains that we were a sausage roll
             short of a full buffet. We'll have to have a word
             with the manager at some stage.

THOMO   (*exasperated*) Frosie, Frosie . . . do we 'ave to!
             Eh? Do we 'ave to go on and on about bloody
             sausage rolls. I mean to say, eh? . . . What are
             we supposed to be 'ere for?

NIGEL   A reunion . . . you know what we're here for.

THOMO   Exactly . . . a reunion. (*Scrabbling about in his
             jacket pocket and producing a dog-eared
             letter.*) In the unforgettable words of your
             invitation to this extravaganza . . . (*He tries to
             read the letter, squinting at it as he moves it
             alternately closer and further away.*) . . .
             what's 'appened to the light in 'ere! 'Ere,
             Frosie . . . read this.

NIGEL   I wrote it!

THOMO   I know you wrote it! Just read it.

NIGEL   I haven't got my reading glasses.

THOMO   Mal . . . 'ere.

MALCOLM   (*taking his spectacles off and fiddling with
             them before putting them back on his nose*)
             Sorry . . . theses are for distance . . . I'm no
             good close up.

THOMO   What a state eh . . . what a bloody state! 'Ere
             Mugsy . . . it'll 'ave to be you. If you're not up
             to it we'll 'ave to 'ave a translation done in
             Braille.

MUGSY   I'll 'ave a go. I'm not right good.

THOMO   Do your best son.

MUGSY   (*reading slowly and carefully*) Dear coll . . .
               eeg . . . yew . . .

THOMO   Dear colleague . . . yes we know all about that
               bit . . . we want the bit at the end.

MUGSY   Right . . . magic. (*Reading again.*) This is a
               great . . . timmy . . . tim . . . time . . . to relieve . . .

NIGEL   . . . relive.

MUGSY   Right . . . relive . . . our shored memories . . .
               and time of slaughter. (MUGSY *looks around at
               them all proudly, only to realise that they are
               all looking back at him in disbelief. He
               quickly glances back at the letter.*) . . . Times
               of laughter.

THOMO   Exactly . . . relive memories . . . laughter eh?
               We're not 'ere to bicker all night about 'ow
               many sausage rolls there were or weren't.
               We're 'ere to continue where we left off
               twenty-five year ago.

MALCOLM   That's exactly what we *are* doing.

THOMO   What do you mean by that?

MALCOLM   I mean we are just continuing where we left off.
               It was always like this. We hardly ever did
               have any laughs. We were always bickering
               and arguing amongst ourselves.

THOMO   No we weren't.

MALCOLM   Yes we were.

THOMO   No we weren't. Are you calling me a liar, eh?
               (*Twitch.*)

NIGEL   Perhaps we might have had the odd word . . .
               occasionally we might have indulged in a little
               jovial banter. Exchanged views. We didn't
               argue.

THOMO   We might 'ave taken the mickey maybe.

MALCOLM   You only took the mickey out of *some* of us.

NIGEL   Only light hearted though.

MALCOLM   To you maybe. My life was miserable. In fact we were all miserable, most of the time.

THOMO   No we weren't! 'Ey, Frosie, you tell 'im. Life and soul of the neighbourhood we were.

MALCOLM   No we weren't.

THOMO   'Ey, Mal . . . shut it, eh? If I say we were 'aving a good time, we were 'aving a good time, eh? (*Twitch.*) All right?

MALCOLM   (*plucking up courage*) You might have had a good time, Thomo. You might have thought it was all right, because you were always on top weren't you. Do this, Mal . . . do that Mal . . . get me another pint or I'll take the piss out of you again in front of everybody. That was your good time wasn't it! Well, maybe I didn't say anything then because I was scared of you . . . but I can say something now because you don't frighten me anymore.

(*There is a stunned silence for several seconds.*)

MUGSY   We 'ad a laugh sometimes though didn't we? It weren't that bad.

NIGEL   Weren't that bad! What are you both talking about? We're here to celebrate the happiest days of our lives. What's got into you, Malcolm? We were a close knit team, we were unbeatable . . . we were like brothers . . . we were *mates*.

MALCOLM   Some of you were mates maybe. Not all of us
               . . . not if we weren't quite perfect. Not if we
               wore glasses, or didn't want to drink until we
               fell over, or were a bit slow with jokes.

THOMO   Or with women.

MALCOLM   And what does that mean?

NIGEL   I don't think we need to go into all that,
               Thomo.

THOMO   Oh no . . . no . . . it's all right for 'im to 'ave a
               go at me is it, eh? (*Twitch.*) No, it's obviously
               time for some 'ome truths. In fact, to tell you
               the truth, Frosie, I'm stunned . . . stunned and
               amazed that 'igh and bloody mighty Malcolm
               'ere should expect us to 'ave been mates with
               'im . . . except I think he's talking about *mates*
               in a bit of a different way to us.

NIGEL   Thomo!

THOMO   No, he's started it . . . it 'as to be said. We all
               know that he never bothered with women don't
               we. We all know about 'im an' Jacko don't we!

MALCOLM   There's no need to bring Jacko into it.

THOMO   Why? Does it surprise you, Mal, that we know
               about you an' 'im?

MUGSY   I don't know owt.

MALCOLM   He was my best friend . . . that's all.

THOMO   'E used to tell us you were always 'anging
               round 'im. Always wanting to make up to 'im.

MALCOLM   That's a lie. Jacko wouldn't have said that.

THOMO   But 'e did.

MALCOLM	Leave him out of it. He understood. He wasn't like you . . . always bullying . . . he was the only real friend I had!
THOMO	Oh, right! But if you don't consider us friends, Malcolm, why did you bother coming 'ere! Why make your life *miserable* again?
MALCOLM	Because I didn't think *you* were going to be here. I was *told* you wouldn't be here. But then you had to turn up and spoil it didn't you . . . like you used to spoil everything. But this time it's not going to work. This time I've got the upper hand.
THOMO	Don't kid yourself, son, don't kid yourself. (THOMO *moves away to the table on which* MALCOLM *put the drinks and sits down. He raises his pint glass to* MALCOLM.) Cheers, Malcolm. Thank you very much.
	(*There is an uneasy silence as* THOMO *takes a long drink of beer.*)
MUGSY	(*eager to restore normality*) Shall I get t' disco going again then?
THOMO	Steady on, Mugs . . . steady. Malcolm's got to tell us all. 'E's going to tell us all why he's got the upper 'and.
NIGEL	No, it's a very good idea that, Mugsy . . . very sound. I think we could all benefit from a little light popular music.
MUGSY	Magic.
	(MUGSY *moves to the disco console and starts to select a record.* MALCOLM *moves over to* THOMO.)
MALCOLM	All right then, Thomo, I'll tell you. You've got me going now, you have. You thought things hadn't changed. Even when we met again after

all that time, the first thing you did was sell me
a pile of rubbish.

THOMO   (*practically speechless*) Rubbish! Eh? That
               were my star bargain o' the week!

MALCOLM   It was a pile of junk, Thomo . . . it was total
               crap. And like usual, I was stupid enough to
               buy it off you. But I'm not as slow as you think
               . . . not anymore . . . not with women? I wasn't
               slow tonight was I? But this time it's me, with
               your woman.

THOMO   Don't let it go to your 'ead, son! Your not
               really 'ere with Lorraine are you! That'd be a
               joke wouldn't it . . . you and 'er. Don't make me
               bloody laugh.

MALCOLM   Oh, I don't think you're going to laugh,
               Thomo. It's not her! No, I arranged to meet
               Shirley here . . . your wife . . . the same as I've
               been meeting her for the last few weeks. What
               do you say to that?

THOMO   You've been doing what!

MALCOLM   I thought that might change things a bit!

THOMO   You bugger . . . you little bugger.

MALCOLM   (*becoming frightened but still defiant*) See . . .
               you don't like it now do you? Not when the
               boot's on the other foot.

               (THOMO *stands, fists clenched, as* MALCOLM
               backs away from him.)

THOMO   When I catch 'old of you, son, the boot won't
               be on the other foot. It'll be all over your
               bloody 'ead!

MALCOLM   What? (*Suddenly terrified.*) Don't, Thomo . . .
               no. I was only joking, honest.

THOMO   Well I'm not laughing am I, eh? (*Twitch.*) I'm
               not laughing, son.

MALCOLM   I can explain it all actually . . . it was quite
               innocent.

THOMO   I'll give you bloody innocence!

               (THOMO *lunges at* MALCOLM *who just manages
               to avoid him.* MALCOLM *runs from the room
               shrieking with fear,* THOMO *closely following
               him, bellowing with rage.*)

MUGSY   (*cheerfully*) Takes you back, doesn't it? Just
               like old times really. Magic.

               (*Rock music blasts out,* MUGSY *head-banging
               to it, as the lights fade.*)

ACT TWO

A little later the same evening. MUGSY *is behind his disco console. He is wearing headphones and seems to be oblivious to anything going on around him as he dances, eyes closed.* SHIRLEY *is sat at one of the tables.* THOMO *paces around the room, agitated.*

THOMO	I don't know 'ow you could do it . . . 'ow could you do it!
SHIRLEY	I haven't done anything really.
THOMO	I mean, any other bloke I could almost understand, but Malcolm? I mean, 'aving an affair with Malcolm when you've already got me . . . it's like . . . it's like . . . it's like, taking a perfectly good spark plug out of your car and replacing it with one that won't fire at all!
SHIRLEY	When you've got a tired old engine it's worth trying anything.
THOMO	And what do you mean by that eh? . . . eh? What do you mean by that?
SHIRLEY	I don't really mean anything. Why are you trying to confuse me . . . talking about cars!
THOMO	Me confuse you . . . me confuse you?
SHIRLEY	And will you stop saying everything twice . . . we'll be here all night.
THOMO	Oh, and you've got other things you'd rather be doing then 'ave you? . . . 'ave you? (*Twitch.*) Well, I'll tell you . . . I'll tell you . . .
SHIRLEY	Look, Thomo . . . it wasn't like that. All Malcolm and me have done is meet up and have the odd drink. Malcolm hasn't tried anything on if that's what you mean. He's not like that.

THOMO   Oh, I know that . . . I know that . . . eh? If
             Malcolm was normal 'e'd 'ave got 'imself a
             woman years ago. 'E wouldn't be wasting 'is
             time messing about wi' you.

SHIRLEY   You're saying I'm a waste of time are you?

THOMO   You're certainly a waste of time to 'im!

SHIRLEY   (*glancing anxiously back at* MUGSY) I don't
             think we should be having this conversation
             really . . . not with Eddie listening.

THOMO   Who?

SHIRLEY   The disco man.

THOMO   That's Mugsy.

SHIRLEY   I know. Eddie Mugsy.

THOMO   No . . . no, Mugsy's 'is nickname.

SHIRLEY   But he's still Eddie.

THOMO   No . . . e's Bernard.

SHIRLEY   Why does he call himself Eddie then?

THOMO   'Cos 'e's a dozy bugger, that's why. Anyway,
             'e can't 'ear anything. In 'is own bloody dream
             world 'e is. The point is . . . what am I going to
             do about Malcolm?

SHIRLEY   You don't need to do anything because
             nothing has happened. Anyway, at least
             Malcolm's the same age as me which is more
             than can be said for you and her!

THOMO   'Er . . . who's 'er?

SHIRLEY   You know perfectly well. I'm not daft, Thomo
             . . . it's quite obvious about you and Lorraine.

THOMO

Me 'an Lorraine! Eh? 'As Malcolm told you that?

SHIRLEY

Oh, he's supposed to cover for you is he . . . but it's not all right for him to have a drink with me? As it happens Malcolm hasn't said anything. For some reason, despite all he's said tonight, he still seems to have some sense of misplaced loyalty towards you. I guessed about Lorraine because you made it very easy for me to guess.

THOMO

Why's that then? Not that I'm saying anything 'as 'appened . . . I don't know 'ow you could think I'd take advantage of that poor innocent girl.

SHIRLEY

I'm not saying that you *have* taken advantage of her . . . I'm saying that you've *tried* to take advantage of her. There's a very big difference as many middle aged men like you have found out.

THOMO

Eh? Well, I 'ave to say, I'm stunned. Eh? Stunned.

SHIRLEY

No you're not, Thomo. You'd only be stunned if you'd actually been successful. We'd *all* have been stunned.

THOMO

What do you mean *all*? Who else knows . . . suspects . . . whatsits? I've been the 'eight of discretion . . . or I would 'ave been . . . 'ad I 'ad anything to be discrete about . . . which I 'aven't.

SHIRLEY

Maybe nobody . . . but *I* knew.

THOMO

'Ow?

SHIRLEY

I can read you like a book, Thomo . . . not a particularly *good* book, not a classic . . . but at least I am still interested enough to dip in to you now and then. I might have got lost with the plot but I do care what happens in the final chapter.

THOMO   What's that supposed to mean eh? Are you calling me a library now!

SHIRLEY   I think it was meant to be a peace offering. We don't have to do this, Thomo. Neither of us needs to be looking elsewhere. We've been through too much together for all of that.

THOMO   You think I'm going to forget . . . just like that!

SHIRLEY   I didn't say either of us could forget . . . but we could forgive. I'm willing to forgive you for Lorraine.

THOMO   Aye well . . . just you keep off Malcolm . . . I'm telling you. And you've no need to go worrying about me . . . I'm not like that. (*Pause, followed by a twitch.*) 'Ow did you know?

SHIRLEY   When a middle aged man who's been married for twenty years suddenly starts cutting his toenails, using aftershave and missing Match of the Day, one instinctively knows . . . oh, and you've started using my hair conditioner and combing your hair differently to try to cover up the bald patch.

THOMO   No I 'aven't.

SHIRLEY   And I do have to say that it wasn't the best choice of aftershave either. You smell like a camel.

             (MALCOLM *peers in through the door cautiously.*)

MALCOLM   Hallo. Everything all right?

SHIRLEY   Yes, Malcolm, I think so.

THOMO   I'm not going to pull your legs off if that's
                 what you mean.

MALCOLM   (*moving in to the room carrying a pint of beer*)
                 I was a little bit worried. I thought you might
                 be upset. I've brought you a pint of best bitter.

MUGSY   (*pulling the headphones off*) Oh you're all
                 right, Mal. They've made up again. 'Ey, did
                 you know Thomo were trying to get off wi'
                 Lorraine? Frosie got it all wrong, you know . . .
                 'e thought she were 'is step-mam.

THOMO   'Ave you been listening!

MUGSY   (*moving away from the console*) No . . . I were
                 listening to these, honest.

                 (*As* MUGSY *moves away from the console, the
                 head phone lead and plug trails behind him.*
                 MUGSY *suddenly realises and looks at it in
                 mock surprise.*)

                 Oh . . . it weren't plugged in! . . . Sorry.

THOMO   Sorry! (*Twitch.*) You *will* be bloody sorry!

MUGSY   (*moving back behind the disco console
                 hurriedly*) No 'arm done though eh? (*Moving a
                 switch.*) 'Ey, do you remember this one?

                 (THOMO'S *face is thunderous as music starts to
                 play and the lights fade. The lights rise stage
                 right to show* NIGEL, THOMO, MALCOLM *and*
                 MUGSY *sitting around a table. In semi-
                 darkness, stage left,* KAY, SHIRLEY, LORRAINE
                 and JENNY *sit around a table. During the
                 following sequence the lights keep cross
                 fading from one group to the other.*)

NIGEL   Right then ladies and gentlemen, if I may have
                 your attention.

MUGSY   There's only gentlemen 'ere!

THOMO   And Malcolm.

NIGEL   All right, it was just a slip of the tongue. Could
            I have your undivided attention please, for a
            few words.

MUGSY   Where are t' ladies anyway?

NIGEL   I don't know. They've gone off to powder their
            noses and do whatever else ladies do when
            they powder their noses. I told Kay I was about
            to start, so if they miss it it's just their own
            hard luck. I'm not waiting any longer.

            (*Lights cross fade to women.*)

LORRAINE   What's t' time?

JENNY   Quarter to ten.

LORRAINE   What are they doing . . . they've been ages
            getting t' drinks. I think it's dead boring wi'
            out men, isn't it?

KAY   Thank you, Lorraine . . . we obviously aren't
            able to stimulate you sufficiently.

LORRAINE   It's just, you need both don't you? Women wi'
            out men . . . it's like strawberries wi' no cream,
            or chips wi' no tomato sauce . . . or chalk wi'
            out cheese.

KAY   I think you're getting a little mixed. Lorraine.
            Chalk and cheese are completely different.

LORRAINE   Yeah . . . so are men an' women. I mean, you
            can 'ave dead interesting talks wi' men . . . you
            know . . . not just about bathrooms and babies
            an' that.

KAY   What would you care for then . . . microbiology
            or sub-atomic particle physics?

LORRAINE	I don't know 'owt about them.
KAY	Oh, really! You surprise me. Anyway, as soon as the men come back I suggest we adjourn to the ladies. Nigel intends giving one of his speeches . . . I think you'd find microbiology a rather refreshing alternative, Lorraine.

(Lights cross fade to men.)

NIGEL	So I would just like to say a few words.
THOMO	You don't usually keep it down to a few!
NIGEL	Thomo please . . . we'll be here all night.
THOMO	That's what I'm frightened of. I know all about you teacher types.
NIGEL	*(irritated)* I'm not a teacher . . . I'm a lecturer.
THOMO	What's the difference?
NIGEL	Well . . . well, teachers teach . . .
THOMO	An' lecturers letch. 'Ey, what's the definition of a lecturer, eh? Eh?
NIGEL	*(resigned)* I don't know. I'm sure you're going to tell me though.
THOMO	A lecturer is somebody who talks in other people's sleep. Get it, eh? Get it? In other people's sleep?
NIGEL	Very good, Thomo. Very funny. Very humorous. Can I get on now?
THOMO	If you 'ave to, son.
NIGEL	Thank you. Now first of all, I know that we are all disappointed not to have a full turn out. I think we can excuse Stinker, because being a Bishop he probably does need to get an early

night on a Saturday. What I do find hard to
credit is the absence of Fatty Smaithwaite,
Bazza and Skegger. I can only propose that,
unless we receive some kind of official
apology, we don't issue them with invitations
to our next reunion twenty-five years hence. I
think that will drive the message home to them
fairly forcibly.

THOMO   Aye . . . they'll be sweating on that one!

NIGEL   Now, the main thrust of my address is a studied
             reflection of major events which we've all been
             privileged to witness during our lives. Now I
             have here a little aide memoire . . .

             (NIGEL *pulls a wad of paper from his pocket as
             the lights cross fade to women.* KAY *is pulling
             a wad of paper from her handbag.*)

KAY   He gave me a reserve copy in case the original
             went astray.

JENNY   (*taking the list from* KAY) He's really going to
             talk about all o' these?

KAY   That's his intention.

JENNY   You've only got t' room booked for one night
             though . . . maybe you should 'ave gone for t'
             whole weekend!

KAY   He seems to think that all these things are
             somehow significant. It took him weeks to
             research it . . . he's been an absolute pain.

             (*Lights cross fade to men.*)

NIGEL   . . . painstaking research, that's the secret. Now
             I'll be placing particular emphasis on the key
             role of technology.

THOMO   Why?

NIGEL   Why? Because *we* are the *children* of the
             technological age. Some generations have been
             privileged to see huge advances in agriculture,
             or the arts, or industry. We've seen
             technology. Think of all the developments in
             our lifetimes.

MALCOLM   He's right.

THOMO   Oh, don't you start as well.

NIGEL   Do you realise, I've got more computing power
             sat on my desk at home than they had for the
             moon landings?

THOMO   You'll be blasting off for Mars when you get
             'ome then, Frosie! You, your paper clips an'
             your desk tidy pen sorter.

NIGEL   You may well mock, Thomo. Thing is . . . where
             would we be today without technology and all
             the benefits it's brought us? Satellite
             navigation systems . . .

MALCOLM   Satellite television.

NIGEL   Life saving surgical equipment . . .

MALCOLM   Organ transplants.

NIGEL   Modern power stations . . .

MUGSY   Electric can openers.

             (*The others look at him in disbelief.*)

NIGEL   I don't think electric can openers are quite in
             the same league that we're talking about here.

MUGSY   But technology's only any use to you if you
             can use it. Electric can openers are dead useful
             . . . especially if you've got loads o' cans you
             want opening.

THOMO	Nice one, son.
NIGEL	All right then, if you like . . . electric can openers.
MUGSY	It makes you wonder doesn't it? 'Ow do things get invented. I mean, 'ow did the wheel get invented?
NIGEL	Well, things like that just happen.
MUGSY	But, say somebody invented a wheel. I mean, 'ow do they know it's a wheel . . . 'ow do they know they 'aven't invented round table tops or summat else that's round!
NIGEL	(*exasperated*) It clearly doesn't work like that, Mugsy. Things like wheels just evolve.
MUGSY	(*smirking*) They what?
NIGEL	Wheels evolve.
MUGSY	(*laughing*) Evolve! 'Ey, did you 'ear that, Thomo?
THOMO	'Ear what?
MUGSY	What Frosie said . . . it were dead funny. It's not like you, Frosie, to get stuff wrong . . . 'cos you're, like, the dead brainy one.
NIGEL	(*indignant*) I haven't got anything wrong!
MUGSY	(*laughing even more*) Yeah, you 'ave . . . you don't even realise do you? (*Hardly able to control himself.*) You said wheels *evolve*.
NIGEL	Yes.
MUGSY	(*almost howling with laughter*) But it's *revolve* isn't it! Wheels *revolve* . . . like with a rrrr.

THOMO   Bloody 'ell, Mugs. God 'elp us!

MUGSY   It's right though isn't it?

NIGEL   Shall we just get on? (*Referring to his papers.*)
                 I think one of the most significant
                 technological triumphs of the early nineties
                 was the launch of the Hubble Space Telescope.
                 I feel this is symbolic of man's gradual taming
                 of the immense forces of the universe.

THOMO   Why are we bothered about that though? We
                 didn't 'ave anything to do with it!

NIGEL   Well, I'm not saying that am I? I'm not saying
                 that we as individuals can take *all* the credit
                 for it. But it was a significant event.

THOMO   Not to us. A significant event to me would be
                 winning t' lottery or pulling a rich bird. A
                 significant event for Malcolm would be a
                 sudden drop in t' price o' semolina or
                 courgettes.

NIGEL   (*getting annoyed*) I'm taking the wider view. If
                 you want something lighter . . . here . . . 1996.
                 Petrol hits £2.40 per gallon.

THOMO   Bloody 'ell.

NIGEL   All right . . . all right . . . 1997. Tony Blair
                 became Prime Minister.

THOMO   I thought we were talking about events, not
                 catastrophe's.

                 (*Lights remain on the men but also rise on the
                 women.*)

JENNY   (*still examining the lists*) I don't think many o'
                 these exactly shaped t' world!

KAY   But that's Nigel . . . obscurity ought to be his
                 middle name.

JENNY	1994. First episode of Time Team.
NIGEL	1998 . . . Apple unveil the iMac.
JENNY	1995 . . . Hot air balloon crosses the Pacific.
KAY	See what I mean! It's a complete and utter waste of time.

(Lights fade on women but remain on the men.)

THOMO	Aye, well, that's all very fine, that's all very good, Frosie, but it's a complete and utter waste o' time. We could be getting on wi' some serious drinking 'ere.
NIGEL	There's more to life than drinking, Thomo. These are the events that have made us what we are . . . the background against which our lives have been shaped . . . the broad canvas on which the detailed brush strokes of life have been painted.
THOMO	All right, all right . . . I've got your gist. I only wanted a simple answer, there's no need to embark on a bloody novel.
NIGEL	These events, Thomo, are our raison d'être.
MALCOLM	No, they're not.
THOMO	Oh, 'ere we go again. What's got into you today, Malcolm! Why can't you just act like normal and keep your mouth shut. It's 'aving my wife . . . it's gone to 'is 'ead!
MALCOLM	I didn't *have* her.
NIGEL	*(quickly)* I think we've already covered that ground. No point in dwelling on the past.
THOMO	We've been dwelling on the past all night!

MALCOLM   All those things . . . world events. None of
           those have changed us. It's not like we've
           been involved in a revolution or a famine or
           something like that. The world has big things
           but we're not big people, we haven't been
           involved . . . we're just very small people living
           very small lives.

THOMO   There's no need to tar us all with the same
           brush. We 'aven't been stacking shelves in the
           Co-op since we left school.

MALCOLM   At least the Co-op's bigger than your
           business.

THOMO   But you don't *own* the Coop do you! That's
           the difference between us, Malcolm . . . you
           work for somebody but I 'ave financial control
           of my own business. It's up 'ere . . . (*Touching
           his head.*) . . . that's what I 'ave to rely on . . .
           whether I sink or swim. I've 'ad to raise a
           family on my mental whatsname . . . support a
           wife and kids.

           (*Lights cross fade to women.*)

SHIRLEY   I don't know how much longer I can cope with
           him really. It's probably my fault, I know. I
           think the trouble is that he resents me and it
           gradually gets worse and worse.

KAY   Why should he resent you?

SHIRLEY   He's always resented the fact that *I* own the
           business.

LORRAINE   He told me it were 'is! He said it were all 'is and
           you were just on the books as a director for tax
           an' that . . . a sleeping partner.

SHIRLEY   Sleeping partner! That's another reason he
           resents me. I sort of went off him . . . after the
           kids. My father gave me the money to set up
           the business . . . he never trusted Thomo.

Things have gradually gone downhill ever
since. When we first started it was all very
grand . . . new premises in a good area. Thomo
was as proud as anything . . . said he was
going to make a real go of it. I was as proud of
him as he was of the business. All we've got
left now is a back street lock-up with Thomo
reduced to palming wrecks off on his supposed
friends. I made him like that. He could have
been a happy family man, with no worries, if
he'd carried on working for somebody else . . .
and I ruined that by expecting so much more.

(*Lights cross fade to men.*)

THOMO   Blood, toil, sweat and tears . . . that's what it's
            taken to build that business up. I started with
            nothing and now look at it. Thompson Motors,
            the name you can trust for 'igh quality and
            reliability at an affordable price.

MUGSY   'Ey . . . I think I'm with you now.

THOMO   Well, that'll be a bloody first, eh . . . I say,
            That'll be a first.

MUGSY   It's that one down Lavender Street isn't it?

THOMO   Aye, that's the one.

MUGSY   It's got big 'oles in t'roof.

THOMO   Temporarily.

MUGSY   And in t'walls.

THOMO   I 'ave 'ad a lot of storm damage of late, yes . . .
            but the cars remain the same 'igh quality.

MUGSY   There were only two in when I passed last
            week.

THOMO   (*twitching*) All right . . . all right . . . I've 'ad a
            bit of a run on 'em.

MALCOLM   Your cars never run at all.

THOMO   (*twitch*) I'm warning you, son.

             (*Lights cross fade to women.*)

SHIRLEY   That's why we had the trouble earlier, you
             know, with Thomo and Mal. I bet you think I'm
             awful, but there wasn't anything in it with Mal
             . . . we just enjoyed going out and, you know,
             doing things. Just normal things really, like
             going to the pictures, or for a little drink . . .
             just the normal things I never do with Thomo.

LORRAINE   I think you do right to go out and enjoy
             yourself. (*Pause.*) You think Thomo's been
             seeing me don't you?

SHIRLEY   I don't blame anybody. It's just the way things
             turn out isn't it.

LORRAINE   I might 'ave seen 'im occasionally . . . like, just
             for a laugh . . . but nothing more than that. 'E's
             not really my type.

SHIRLEY   (*making a rare attempt at a joke*) He's not
             really anybody's type.

             (*She giggles at her joke rather falsely. The
             others look at her.*)

             (*now self conscious*) Sorry. (*Pause.*) Malcolm
             and I only wanted company . . . it was just a
             chance to cheer each other up.

             (*Lights cross fade to men.*)

MALCOLM   We've all wasted any chances we've ever had.

THOMO   'Ey up, 'e's off again!

MALCOLM   Why shouldn't I say what I think! Why do you
             hate me so much, Thomo?

THOMO   Me? I don't 'ate you as such . . . you just get
             on my nerves. There's nothing wrong with that
             is there?

MALCOLM   Why couldn't you ever accept me for what I
             am? You think that, just because I've spent
             years doing a routine job in a routine place, I
             can't think . . . that I'm dull. Well what if I am?
             It's people like you who've made me dull. I've
             never done anything with my life because
             nobody ever let me join in. You never let me
             join in with anything because you thought I
             was a bit different . . . a bit soft.

THOMO   Aye, well you *were* different. We all know that.

MALCOLM   Why don't you come out and say what you
             mean, Thomo? Say the word. You keep skirting
             round it. Shall I use it for you? You think I'm a
             poof don't you . . . a queer?

NIGEL   Steady on, Malcolm!

MALCOLM   No. He wants to hear it, don't you? What other
             words would you call it, Thomo? A fairy? A . . .
             a . . . a . . . a pansy . . . that's it isn't it? You
             think I'm a big pansy?

             (THOMO *for once remains in embarrassed
             silence.*)

             Well I can tell you, Thomo . . . as it happens
             I'm none of those. But if I were I wouldn't be
             ashamed of it . . . I'd still be the same me! So
             what about Jacko and me? Yes I did hang
             around him if you must know . . . and yes, I
             even hero-worshipped him a bit . . . but only
             because I knew where I was with Jacko. He let
             me be me . . . and he liked me for it . . . faults
             and all. So don't try to tell me how great you all
             are . . . don't try to make me feel inadequate.
             Jacko's the only one of us who would have led
             a *big* life . . . an *important* life . . . because he's

the only one of us who *understood* life. He's the only one who really cared.

(*There is a complete silence for several seconds.*)

THOMO So you're not, you know, one o' them? Not a, whatsname . . . an uphill skier?

(*There is another silence as* MALCOLM *returns* THOMO'S *gaze defiantly.*)

Well, I may 'ave been a bit 'arsh on you, Malcolm . . . a bit over 'arsh, maybe, on reflection. No real 'arm meant by it . . . but it does 'ave to be said that you still get right up my nose. Sorry, son.

MALCOLM Apology accepted. You get up my nose as well.

THOMO Aye, well, that's only fair . . . no 'ard feelings about that.

NIGEL Good. Well done. I'm glad we've cleared the air a bit . . . resolved the little differences. Group therapy, that's the thing . . . marvellous. Though I must say I certainly can't agree with your philosophy, Mal, apropos of Jacko being the only one of us destined for greatness. Take Stinker for example.

THOMO Aye, but anybody could be a Bishop. You just 'ave to say a lot o' prayers and do your best to look an 'armless old git.

NIGEL Well, all right then, take *me*. Most people, I think, would regard me as something of a success story. University education . . .

MALCOLM You went to a Technical College!

NIGEL Yes, but the point is, Mal, it's a University now! As I was saying, a Higher National Diploma, which led me on to a fairly meteoric

rise through the ranks of Local Government . . .
many were tipping me to fast-track to the very
top . . . senior clerical officer.

(NIGEL *pauses for a reaction, but receives
none.*)

Yes, I thought that would surprise you. Allied
to that there's my ten years service in Further
Education . . . teaching, developing, moulding,
facilitating. You probably hadn't realised it but
you're talking to the man who got a new part
time certificate in Small Business Bookkeeping
off the ground almost single handed. I think all
in all we're looking at the profile of a fairly
adequate success story there, Malcolm . . . not
perhaps the curriculum vitae of a Ghandi or an
Obama, but hardly what I would call a *small*
life.

(*Lights cross fade to women.*)

KAY

Perhaps you shouldn't be too hard on your
husband, Shirley. He has at least managed to
stay afloat, which is no mean feat these days.
I'd always hoped that Nigel might have gone
much further, but he's rather too parochial . . .
always had to seek the comfort and shelter of
large autocratic organisations. Oh no, I don't
think Nigel would stay afloat on his own.

JENNY

Maybe what you're all forgetting is a bit of
support for 'em! All I've 'eard you doing is
pulling your men apart! Maybe there's more to
a relationship than that.

KAY

Don't get me wrong, Jenny. I'm the most
supportive of wives, but I do believe that a
good marriage is an equal partnership in which
the woman must establish firm control. I'd be
the first to acknowledge Nigel's strengths . . .
(*Short pause as she fails to think of any.*) . . .
but by the same token we must be aware of
weaknesses. Now, one of Nigel's principal

weaknesses is that he's always tended to hide
behind convention since he was dragged,
rather reluctantly, from his mother's womb.
Those who are bound by convention rarely
succeed in any entrepreneurial sense. Are you
following me, Jenny?

JENNY   Just about yes. You're very keen on words wi'
           lots of syllables aren't you?

KAY   I have had the benefit of a *private* education if
           that's what you mean.

JENNY   In *my* education I learnt that over-complication
           can lead to lack of communication.

KAY   Well, that sounds very grand. Lorraine was
           telling me earlier about her GCSE . . . you have
           one as well, Jenny?

JENNY   Yeah.

           (KAY *looks suitably triumphant.*)

           And a PhD in Digital Communication and Data
           Transfer Systems. (*Smiling as she raises her
           glass.*) Cheers.

           (KAY *is deflated, uncertain how to react as the
           lights cross fade to the men.*)

NIGEL   Above all though, Malcolm, and this is very
           important, I've endeavoured to ensure that I
           retained the common touch. The ability to
           communicate at all levels . . . that's a very
           important leadership quality. No, I think if you
           were to ask Kay whether I'd led a small life,
           she'd be pretty much lost for words.

MALCOLM   You don't understand what I'm saying do you?
           We haven't been affected by anything *big* in
           our lives. Twenty-five years on we can come
           back here and carry on where we left off . . . it's

as though nothing has happened in between. What's the point of that?

THOMO   We're not allowed to enjoy ourselves then! There's nothing wrong wi' 'aving a pint with your mates.

MALCOLM   But that's what I said before. We're not mates and we never have been. Look at you three. On the surface you might get on some of the time but underneath it all I doubt whether you even like each other . . . you probably never did.

MUGSY   I don't think you're right there, Mal. We've always been mates . . . it's right important that.

THOMO   Good point well made, Mugs. Very astute.

MUGSY   Aye.

THOMO   Three of us can't be wrong can we, Mal? Maybe it's just you that's out of step, eh? Even Mugsy can see that and he's as daft as a brush . . . he wasn't even one of us.

MUGSY   Yeah, I were.

THOMO   Not properly though, Mugs . . . not like the rest of us.

MUGSY   (*smiling uncertainly in confusion*) Yeah, I were . . . weren't I Mal? . . . weren't I Frosie?

            (*They remain in embarrassed silence.*)

            I used to come 'ere with the rest of you.

THOMO   I'm not denying that, son . . . but you weren't one of *us* were you . . . not officially . . . not one of the Magnificent Eight.

NIGEL   Strictly speaking, Mugs, he is right.

THOMO   I mean you're only here by accident tonight
             aren't you? Because of yer disco. You weren't
             invited. You just turned up 'ere like a bad
             penny . . . same as you always did.

MUGSY   Frosie didn't know where I was.

THOMO   But he found everybody else! He could 'ave
             found you couldn't he, but he didn't bother.
             Don't get me wrong . . . we don't mind you
             being 'ere . . . as it turns out it's a bloody
             blessing wi' all that food to pay for.

MUGSY   But I always belonged 'ere wi' you. We always
             used to 'ave a right good laugh, didn't we? I
             were the same as you . . . we *were* mates and
             we did 'ave a good time.

THOMO   Malcolm doesn't seem to think so.

MUGSY   But 'e's not right. Just 'cos he used to be
             miserable . . . that's not my fault. I were always
             friendly wi' you weren't I, Mal?

MALCOLM   Yes, I suppose so . . . *you* were.

MUGSY   (*increasingly agitated*) And you're wrong
             about all those other things . . . *big* things. I
             saw some of 'em. I were there. I were in Iraq.

MALCOLM   I didn't know that.

MUGSY   There's a lot you don't know . . . any of you.
             You all keep going on as though you know
             everything, but you don't.

THOMO   So what do you know then, Mugs, eh? What do
             you know that we don't?

             (*There is a pause as* MUGSY *gathers his
             thoughts.*)

MUGSY   I know people laugh at me . . . 'cos I'm a bit
             slow. I can't 'elp that. When I joined t' army it

were the same. They said I were thick 'cos it
took me a bit to learn things. They didn't call
me Mugsy . . . they called me crap 'ead 'cos,
like, they said my 'ead was full o' crap.

THOMO   Soon got your measure then, 'ey, son?

MUGSY   I didn't mind though 'cos I kept telling meself,
they don't matter, these aren't my *real* mates
. . . my real mates are back at 'ome. (*Pause.*) It's
never like you think it will be. I always thought
it looked dead good in films, dead exciting . . .
like you shot at people and they just fell over
and you felt dead good . . . like being a 'ero.
It's not like that. Proper people don't always
fall over like that. Sometimes they just run
around screaming and you can see bits coming
out of 'em . . . you don't know what bits they
are 'cos you're not a doctor . . . but . . . (*Pause,
becoming increasingly agitated.*) One day we
were clearing some trenches . . . taking
prisoners like. I don't know 'ow it 'appened but
I got separated from t'rest and ended up in this
bunker. It were dead dark and scary and I were
trying to get out . . . suddenly this towel 'ead
were there . . . this Iraqi. He was just there, out
of nowhere . . . coming at me wi' a knife . . . I
could see it glinting in 'is 'and. I fired but I'd
left t'safety on, so I panicked, I didn't know
what to do. I stuck me bayonet in 'im . . . I 'ad
to really, I didn't 'ave any choice 'cos 'e
wouldn't run away . . . 'e should 'ave run away.
He were looking at me as I were doing it . . .
like, just staring at me . . . into my eyes, he
couldn't believe it . . . and then (*Making wild,
violent stabbing motions.*) I just kept on doing
it 'cos I didn't know what else to do. If I'd
stopped I'd 'ave 'ad to 'elp 'im, and I couldn't
'ave 'cos I'm too stupid, I'd 'ave got it all
wrong . . . I 'ad to kill 'im . . . I 'ad to stop 'im
staring. (*Pause.*) When it were all finished, I
saw . . . he didn't 'ave a knife at all. It were a
tin can. 'E'd been offering me some food to
show he was friendly . . . He'd been even more

scared than me. (*Pause.*) When the rest o' my
lot found me I were just throwing up . . . I
couldn't stop. I couldn't forget 'is eyes . . . like
he couldn't understand what was 'appening.
Some of 'em just laughed at me . . . but I
thought, it doesn't matter, they're not real
mates. Real mates wouldn't laugh like that. Not
when they saw what I'd done.

(*Lights cross fade to the women.*)

JENNY   He got a medical discharge soon after that. He
doesn't often talk about it. I'm sure telling
people would 'elp 'im, but 'e's got this thing
about it. I think he'd 'ave to feel really close to
somebody . . . really trust them.

SHIRLEY   Is this where you met him? You working behind
the bar and him with his discotheque. He seems
to really enjoy that.

JENNY   Oh, 'is disco's just a bit of a 'obby really . . .
one of t' perks o' job he calls it. Didn't he tell
you? He's 'opeless sometimes. He doesn't just
work 'ere, he owns it . . . this and another two
of 'em.

(*Lights go up on the men as well.*)

THOMO   'Ow many!

MUGSY   Another two of 'em. I do disco's in 'em all . . .
it's magic.

JENNY   He had a small win on a scratchcard and
bought a part share in this one. Since then,
everything 'e touches seems to turn to gold.
Quite the businessman when 'e puts 'is mind to
it.

THOMO   Bloody 'ell!

(*The lights fade and music plays. The lights
rise to find* SHIRLEY, LORRAINE *and* MALCOLM

dancing. KAY *is sat to one side watching.*
THOMO *and* NIGEL *are sat at the same table as*
KAY, *in earnest discussion. After a few seconds*
the music stops.)

LORRAINE   That were great, Mal. You're a right good
            dancer aren't you?

MALCOLM   I wouldn't say that.

LORRAINE   I know you wouldn't. That's why *I* said it. (*To*
            everyone.) Where's Mugsy gone, we need
            another record?

SHIRLEY   I think he and Jenny have gone to give the bar
            staff a hand with 'last orders'.

LORRAINE   But we need another record on!

THOMO   That'll wait. We 'ave important things to
            discuss.

NIGEL   We ought to have you in on this one, Mal. We
            need a quorum.

LORRAINE   Oh, *I* eat that. I don't think it's right to eat
            animals do you? Come on, Shirley, lets 'ave a
            look for a record.

            (SHIRLEY *and* LORRAINE *move onto the platform*
            and look through the records. MALCOLM *moves*
            towards the table.)

THOMO   Well sit down then, Malcolm, don't stand there
            making the place look untidy.

MALCOLM   (*sitting*) Who'd have thought it . . . Mugsy
            being a war hero?

THOMO   Nobody says he was a 'ero, son, let's not get
            carried away. The important thing, though, is
            that he fought for 'is country, even if it was
            just against a bloke armed with a tin o' Spam.
            Now we 'ave a proposal . . .

NIGEL   Excuse me, Thomo, I thought we agreed that I'd
               chair this one . . . having had rather more
               experience of the corporate decision making
               process.

THOMO   Bloody 'ell, carry on then . . . we're 'ardly
               Unilever are we!

NIGEL   Thank you. Now we 'ave . . . *have* a proposal
               on the table. The proposal is that Mugsy be
               made an honorary member of the Magnificent
               Eight. Now strictly speaking that would make it
               the Magnificent Nine, but for the purposes of
               continuity we would continue to be called the
               Magnificent Eight.

THOMO   Which would be acceptable you see, there only
               being seven of us at the moment . . . due to the
               demise of Jacko and 'is motorbike in
               unfortunate and tragic circumstances.

NIGEL   How do you feel about that, Mal? Should we
               continue to be a factual seven but still called
               eight, eight in name and number, or eight in
               number but nine in name as a mark of respect to
               Jacko?

KAY   Have you heard yourselves!

NIGEL   What's wrong with that? I think you'll find the
               mathematics impeccable, my love.

KAY   I'm not talking about the mathematics.

NIGEL   So what do you think, Mal?

KAY   There's poor Mister Mugsy, desperate for
               friendship and you have to reduce it to this.

NIGEL   I'm sorry, my love, but we are in the middle of a
               meeting here . . . a very important meeting and
               I've been charged with the task of keeping it to
               order. I can't have these interruptions.

THOMO	'Ere, 'ere.
NIGEL	Through the chair, Thomo, please.
THOMO	Through the chair, 'ere. 'ere.
NIGEL	Thank you.
THOMO	We're not just talking about friends 'ere, we're talking about mates. There is a difference.
KAY	I am aware, yes.
THOMO	Now, the biggest stumbling block, as I see it, is the initiation ceremony.
MALCOLM	I hated that.
THOMO	Well, you would do, it were never a pretty sight, I know . . . but that was the point . . . it made men of us . . . some of us anyway.
NIGEL	So why is it a problem?
THOMO	Well, we no longer 'ave the original official lavatory brush . . . I don't think, strictly speaking, that it would be possible to conduct a valid ceremony with a replacement lavatory brush.
NIGEL	Well, that's it then?
THOMO	Unless, of course, it were a very well used one. We could probably get away wi' that.
NIGEL	Agreed. So we have a proposal from the floor re the initiation of Mugsy. Do we have a second?
MALCOLM	(looking at his watch) We've got about an hour I think.
NIGEL	A seconder for the proposal!

MALCOLM	Oh, yes, definitely.
NIGEL	Go on then.
MALCOLM	I second the proposal.
THOMO	So we go for it then?
NIGEL	Those in favour say aye.
THOMO	Aye.
MALCOLM	Aye.
NIGEL	Those against say nay . . .
MALCOLM	Nay. (NIGEL *and* THOMO *glare at him in disbelief.*) Sorry . . . Got a bit confused.
NIGEL	The aye's have it then, motion carried. I declare the meeting closed. (*To* KAY.) That's it then, he's in . . . or he will be very shortly.
KAY	Bravo.
THOMO	'Ang on, 'ang on, the meeting isn't properly closed yet. We didn't do the . . . (*Hesitant to say it in front of* KAY.)
NIGEL	Didn't do what?
THOMO	The . . . you know . . . the whatsname . . . (*Almost whispering.*) . . . secret 'andshake. We always had to finish a meeting wi' that, otherwise it weren't official.
NIGEL	But surely we don't need to now . . . it's a long time ago . . . thing is . . . (*Trying to point discretely to* KAY.) . . . it's a bit, you know.
THOMO	Well, if you don't want it done properly, officially, on your 'ead be it.

NIGEL   Ah . . . yes. (*Hesitant.*) Kay, my sweet.
            (*Uncertain how to tell* KAY.) The thing is,
            you'll have to look away, please.

KAY   Why?

NIGEL   While we do the secret handshake.

KAY   Oh my God! Why can't I watch?

NIGEL   Then it wouldn't be secret would it!

KAY   I promise I won't tell anyone.

NIGEL   That's not the point!

KAY   What if I refuse to look away . . . what will you
            do then?

NIGEL   We'll probably have to retire to the
            gentlemen's convenience, which would be
            rather *inconvenient* as it happens. Kay, please,
            I am asking you nicely . . . as my wife . . .
            please?

KAY   Oh, very well. (*Moving away to nibble at
            crisps on the buffet.*) It really is pathetic, you
            realise that . . . grown men with secret
            handshakes? Are you affiliated to the Masons?

            (NIGEL, THOMO *and* MALCOLM *watch her move
            away, then glance anxiously over their
            shoulders to make sure that* LORRAINE *and*
            SHIRLEY *aren't watching. They are still
            looking carefully through records.*)

THOMO   Right. Shall I take t' lead?

NIGEL   Quick as you can, Thomo.

            (NIGEL, THOMO *and* MALCOLM *stand in a semi-
            circle and hold out their right hands, clasping
            each others right hands in front of their semi-
            circle.*)

THOMO   (*chanting*) By t'eye of t'frog and t'creak of
                         t'gates, we vow we'll always 'elp our mates.
                         We make this pledge, by t' secret sign, may
                         those who break it 'ope to die.

                         (*They put their left hands up to their noses,
                         touching the tips of their noses with their
                         thumbs and waggling their fingers and they
                         all chant "Oggle oggle oggle". They
                         immediately separate hands and put both their
                         hands up to the sides of their heads like ears
                         and waggle their fingers as they squeak "Eek
                         eek eek". The ceremony completed, they all
                         step back fairly quickly, trying hard to be very
                         casual and manly but obviously embarrassed.*
                         THOMO *twitches.*)

NIGEL   All right now my love.

KAY   Oh, I'm so glad. I was feeling a little
                         marginalised, not knowing the secret sign.
                         What happens now? Do you all dash off and
                         tell each other ripping yarns round a camp fire?

NIGEL   Very funny, Kay . . . yes, very humorous.

KAY   Yes, well, it is from where I'm standing!

                         (JENNY *enters looking worried.*)

JENNY   There's going to be trouble wi' Mugsy.

THOMO   Not any more, he's in . . . we've 'ad a vote.

JENNY   What?

THOMO   'E's officially one of us now, or 'e will be when
                         we've conducted the ceremony. There's no
                         going back on it 'cos it's been sealed wi' t'
                         sacred oath. You don't 'ave an old lavatory
                         brush 'andy do you?

JENNY   No, I mean there's going to be trouble in t' bar!
             It's a couple o' lads. It's 'appened before . . .
             they come in and pick a fight wi' Mugsy 'cos
             of the way he is. He won't fight back . . . not
             after the army.

NIGEL   Oh dear . . . oh dear, oh dear. Hadn't you better
             call the police?

JENNY   Oh, they're no good. It'll all be over by the
             time they arrive!

NIGEL   What about the bar staff?

JENNY   We've only got young lasses on . . . they can't
             do 'owt to 'elp 'im.

NIGEL   (*panicking*) Right then . . . this calls for
             decisive action . . . thing is, don't panic . . . I'll
             handle this. Yes, that'll be best. What we need
             to do is make some decisions fast. Not hasty
             ones mind. Maybe we need to convene another
             meeting.

THOMO   Aye . . . we'll sort it, won't we lads?

NIGEL   Right then. I'd like to formally reconvene the
             meeting. Now I think the first consideration
             is . . .

THOMO   No, I mean *we'll* sort it out. We've always
             looked after our own 'aven't we!

MALCOLM   That was a long time ago, Thomo. Anyway, I
             can't remember you ever helping me.

THOMO   That, Mal, was because you never got into any
             trouble . . . you always moved like a whippet
             when it suited you. Usain Bolt in a duffle coat.

JENNY   Will you just do *something*!

THOMO	Aye, we will do . . . when I can just get Malcolm stirred into a bit of action! Just the two of 'em you said?
JENNY	Yeah.
THOMO	There you go Frosie, we can sort that out. Are you with me lads or not!
JENNY	An' another three or four of their mates.
THOMO	Right. I'm with you now . . . right. (*Twitch.*) Alternatively, you may well 'ave a point, Frosie. It might be worth giving t'police a call as they could just be 'aving a bit of a lull at the moment.
JENNY	What! You're bloody useless all of you . . . are you going to carry on letting 'im down for the rest of your lives! I'm going back to 'elp 'im.
	(JENNY *runs out. There is silence for several seconds.*)
NIGEL	A bit of an over reaction there I think. No point in going over the top. The art of crisis management is to keep a cool head at times like this, that's the important thing.
THOMO	Aye, right over t' top. Maybe we should pop outside, Frosie. A spot of fresh air might 'elp us think clearer. Mal can 'old the fort 'ere.
NIGEL	Good idea, Thomo. (*To* KAY, *finally decisive.*) I'll see you in a few minutes my love. Don't worry about me, I'll be all right. We'll go out the back way where it's a bit quieter.
	(NIGEL *and* THOMO *move towards the door. They are pulled up short by* KAY.)
KAY	Is that it! Is that all you're going to do?
NIGEL	As I said . . . there's no need to worry yourself.

KAY   You're going to leave poor Mister Mugsy and
            Jenny to cope in there on their own! After all
            you've been going on about *mates*! What sort
            of *mates* are you then!

NIGEL   Steady, Kay . . . bit unlike you.

KAY   All three of you . . . you're so wrapped up in
            how things were . . . how wonderful you all
            were. Why don't you face reality for a change
            . . . face the reality of what's happening here
            and now. That poor man needs your help.

NIGEL   I don't know what's got into you, my love.
            Why don't you sit down . . . have one of your
            tablets. You're over-exciting yourself.

KAY   Over-exciting myself! I can tell you here and
            now in front of witnesses that I have had no
            reason whatsoever to get over-excited in the
            last twenty years of being married to you.

NIGEL   Oh, yes, very good, Kay . . . very humorous.

KAY   I was not being humorous . . . and what's more
            I'm bloody sick of you always saying "very
            humorous". I am not a humorous person
            because you give me nothing to be humorous
            about. We have forgotten how to laugh, Nigel.

THOMO   I think you're being a bit 'arsh there, Kay . . .
            'is one liners are very good.

KAY   All you do is talk. You talk endlessly about
            how you *manage* things . . . how you *do* things
            . . . but you never actually *manage* to *do*
            anything. I'm sorry, Nigel but it has to be said.
            You can reminisce for all you're worth about
            how you used to be "Jack the lad", but sooner
            or later you're going to have to face up to the
            fact that you are now a boring, middle-aged,
            middle-class windbag with thinning hair,

thinning teeth and a rapidly thinning veneer of credibility.

(*Pause.*)

NIGEL   (*hurt*) I gather you're not one hundred percent behind my plan then?

KAY   Stop planning . . . start doing.

THOMO   Very 'arsh!

SHIRLEY   And you're no better!

THOMO   What!

SHIRLEY   You're so busy living in the past you forget how to live for the future. It's time to start enjoying ourselves *now*. I thought you used to like a fight.

THOMO   Of a Saturday night, yes.

SHIRLEY   Well, it's Saturday night now.

THOMO   But when we started courting you made me stop!

SHIRLEY   I made you stop all sorts of things but you've gradually started doing them all again!

THOMO   You wouldn't mind then? I'm out of practice.

SHIRLEY   I'm sure it's like riding a bike. And I think you should join them, Mal.

MALCOLM   Me! I never enjoyed a fight. (*Glum.*) In fact I never enjoyed anything much at all.

LORRAINE   (*suddenly inspired*) That's it then. It's up to all of you to make this the full stop to your past and the capital letter of a new paragraph of your future. That's good isn't it . . . I thought that out all by meself!

KAY   If Mugsy's a mate, as you suddenly now claim, you should be in there with him.

               (NIGEL, THOMO and MALCOLM *look at each other, finally stung into action.*)

THOMO   Right . . . let's do it

               (*The three of them walk purposefully towards the door. Just before they reach it,* THOMO *stops, pretending to tie his shoelace and* NIGEL *gives way to* MALCOLM *at the door.*)

NIGEL   After you, Mal.

MALCOLM   No it's all right. (*Noticing* THOMO.) What are you doing, Thomo?

THOMO   Bloody lace. Carry on lads . . . I'll be right behind you when I've done this.

SHIRLEY   Thomo, you're wearing slip-ons!

THOMO   Am I? Bloody 'ell, so I am! (*Twitch.*) All right . . . I'm going. (THOMO *stands and moves to the door. Twitching.*) Right.

LORRAINE   (*excited*) It's just like one o' those films isn't it . . . where the 'ero's walk shoulder to shoulder in to t' sunset . . . an' they all get killed . . . all except one who comes 'ome to marry 'is true love.

THOMO   Oh, thank you very much. That's a comfort isn't it, lads!

NIGEL   (*nervous*) See you soon then, love.

KAY   You give it to them, Tiger.

NIGEL   Oh yes . . . very good, very humorous.

               (NIGEL, THOMO and MALCOLM *exit.*)

LORRAINE   (*shouting after them*) You stick one on 'em,
                Mal.

                (*There is silence and the three of them look at
                each other uncertainly.*)

KAY   I can't believe I've just done that.

SHIRLEY   I think we got carried away.

KAY   Nigel couldn't fight his way out of a paper bag
                . . . even armed with a pair of scissors.

SHIRLEY   Maybe we should go and fetch them back. It's
                not too late to get the police.

                (*There is a sudden brief commotion outside
                with shouting and crashing noises.*)

                Or maybe it is.

LORRAINE   They'll be all right. Your Thomo once told me
                he used to be an amateur boxing champ.

SHIRLEY   You don't believe everything he says do you?

                (*There is another flurry of noise in the
                background, followed by a loud crash.* THOMO
                *staggers backwards along the corridor, past
                the door. He reappears a moment later and
                stands in the doorway.*)

THOMO   (*shouting down the corridor*) 'Ey, try that once
                more and our lad wi' specs'll 'ave you! 'E
                might not look much but 'e's dynamite when
                'e's roused . . . (*Twitching once then entering
                the room. He finishes his previous sentence
                more quietly to himself.*) . . . it's never
                'appened yet mind but we live in 'ope. Where's
                me pint?

SHIRLEY   What are you doing back here?

| THOMO | I left me pint didn't I . . . can't 'ave a decent scrap wi'out a pint. 'Ey, pass me one of those sausage rolls as well. |

(SHIRLEY *moves to fetch him a sausage roll from the table.*)

| LORRAINE | Shouldn't you be in there sorting 'em out? |

| THOMO | Oh, it 'asn't got started yet. Just the initial skirmishing. (*Twitch.*) |

| KAY | (*passing* THOMO *his pint*) What's happening then? |

| THOMO | Well your Frosie opened negotiations, 'oping for a peaceful settlement of the dispute. They've tabled an opposing view . . . in fact the table *was* the opposing view, in that they threw it at Frosie. |

| KAY | Is he . . . ? |

| THOMO | Oh, he's all right, 'opeless shot, they missed 'im by a mile . . . it gave Mal a nasty crack though, which is a disappointment as we'd designated 'im as our reserve rapid reaction force! |

(SHIRLEY *gives him a sausage roll.*)

Right, best get back then. They're big lads you know . . . especially t' two I'm leaving to Frosie!

(*As* THOMO *moves towards the door,* SHIRLEY *suddenly runs after him and gives him a peck on the cheek.*)

| SHIRLEY | Good luck, love. |

| THOMO | (*surprised*) Aye . . . thanks, pet . . . thank you very much. (*Twitch.*) |

(THOMO *strides out of the door*)

SHIRLEY   His heart's in the right place you know. It's just that he's a bit of a pratt.

KAY   Aren't they all, Shirley, aren't they all.

           (*There is a sudden commotion outside the door which goes on for quite some time. With every crash and bang, the women wince, glancing at each other. Finally the noise subsides slightly and a bottle whistles past the doorway, shortly followed by* NIGEL *who stops in the doorway looking back down the corridor.*)

NIGEL   (*shouting back down the corridor*) Now just you stop that right now . . . (NIGEL *ducks and a bottle flies over his head along the corridor. He stands again.*) I won't ask you again. I said stop that or you'll be very sorry I can tell you. (*Stepping in through the doorway, looking very flustered.*) I'd stay in here if I were you ladies, it's livening up out there now.

KAY   I'm sorry, Nigel, I didn't mean to send you out there. You're not *all* that boring honestly . . . just *some* of the time.

NIGEL   Oh, well . . . thank you, my sweet. Thing is . . . bit late now, having sent me out into that maelstrom. Very nice sentiment though. I shall bear it in mind . . . give me something to reflect on while I'm lying in hospital.

KAY   Oh, don't be so dramatic.

NIGEL   They're throwing bottles! How dramatic do you want it! One of them hit Mugsy . . . fortunately he took most of the pace off it with his head so there's not too much damage done.

KAY   Perhaps you should throw some bottles back.

NIGEL   What! I can't believe you said that. You know
                my views on ecology. Bottles should be safely
                desposed of in an environmentally friendly way
                in the bottle bank.

KAY   Get mean, Nigel. For once in your life, go for it.

NIGEL   Suppose I could try. Thing is . . . (*Hopefully.*)
                did you really mean Tiger?

KAY   Of course I did.

NIGEL   Oh! Jolly good.

                (NIGEL *steps out of the doorway and
                immediately ducks, just before a bottle
                whistles past him. He stands again.*)

                I said stop that. You're not listening to me are
                you.

                (NIGEL *steps off back down the corridor and
                the commotion grows louder again. The girls
                return to wincing at the crashes. Suddenly
                MUGSY appears running down the corridor
                and straight into the room. He is grinning
                broadly and is pulling THOMO behind him,
                having thrown a bar towel over his head and
                clamped his head under his arm in a head
                lock. It is not possible to see THOMO's face.*)

MUGSY   'Ey, it's right good this . . . I'm gonna pull this
                one's 'ead off in a minute if 'e's not careful.

                (THOMO *struggles violently, grunting loudly.*
                MUGSY *responds by slapping him on top of the
                head with his free hand.*)

                Shut up you . . . I weren't talking to you!

KAY   Jenny said you didn't fight anymore!

MUGSY   Oh, I wouldn't fight but this isn't like fighting,
            is it? It's just 'aving a good time wi' yer mates.
            It's magic.

            (THOMO *grunts again.*)

            I said *you* 'ad to shut up!

THOMO   It's me you daft pillock.

LORRAINE   'Ey, it's Thomo. You look right funny like that,
            Thomo.

THOMO   Just get this daft bugger off me will you!

MUGSY   Thomo? (*Letting him go.*) 'Ow did you get
            there?

THOMO   (*standing and checking that his head is still
            on his shoulders*) You put me there you silly
            sod! I'm meant to be on your side you know!

MUGSY   I know. I thought I'd got one o' *them*! (*To the
            women.*) It's dead funny that isn't it? (*To
            THOMO.*) I thought you were one o' them.

THOMO   (*twitch*) Well I wasn't was I?

SHIRLEY   How's it going, love?

THOMO   (*pausing to consider*) Well, let's just say that
            if it were a football match we'd be looking for a
            vast improvement in the second 'alf. (*To
            MUGSY.*) Come on, let's 'ave you back in there,
            son.

MUGSY   Yeah . . . I'll go and get one o' *them* now.

            (THOMO *leads* MUGSY *back off.*)

            (*turning with a parting shot*) It's magic is this.

            (MUGSY *disappears from view. The sounds of
            fighting grow louder and more frantic.*

LORRAINE *cautiously moves to the door and peers out.*)

LORRAINE   I don't think they're doing right well out there.

KAY   There's only one thing for it then.

(KAY *picks up her handbag, swings it by the strap against her other hand and decides that it is not heavy enough. She empties the contents onto a table and replaces them with some empty bottles, test swings it again and smiles in satisfaction.*)

Are you with me?

SHIRLEY   We can't go in there!

KAY   Why not? This is going to come as somewhat of a surprise to Nigel, but before I met him I led a rather adventurous social life. Just stick with me.

LORRAINE   Well, I'm with you. (*Removing one of her stilettos and grasping it by the sole in her hand.*) I 'ate bullies.

(KAY *and* LORRAINE *exit with determined expressions.* SHIRLEY *looks after them for a second, then makes a decision. She looks round, picks up the trifle from the table and exits. Music plays as the sound of fighting dies and the lights fade. The music fades and the lights rise to find* NIGEL, MALCOLM *and* THOMO *sitting, nursing their wounds.* NIGEL *has an arm in a sling,* MALCOLM *has his head bandaged, whilst* THOMO *keeps prodding tenderly at a plaster, just below his eye.* MUGSY *is stood next to them, grinning.* LORRAINE, KAY *and* SHIRLEY *are all unscathed and are standing together in a group, talking.* JENNY *enters carrying a cloth containing some ice which she gives to* THOMO.)

JENNY   That'll 'elp t' swelling.

THOMO   I don't think it needs any 'elp . . . it's blowing
               up quite well by itself. I wouldn't mind but I
               were untouched 'til 'e got 'old o' me.

MUGSY   It were a dead good 'ead lock that weren't it!

JENNY   I thought it was great the way everybody got
               stuck in to 'elp you out. (*To* NIGEL, MALCOLM
               and THOMO.) Sorry you three ended up at t'
               'ospital though. 'Ow are you feeling now?

MALCOLM   Much better thanks . . . I can only see three of
               everything now, so that's a bit of an
               improvement.

LORRAINE   They should've kept you in . . . you might have
               concussion. You should 'ave told 'em, Mal.

THOMO   I'll tell you one thing, those other lads knew
               they'd been in a scrap. I've never seen an
               'andbag cause so much damage.

KAY   My aim was rather *in* wasn't it? I used to play a
               lot of rounders in my teens.

NIGEL   But, the main thing is, I think they will now
               appreciate the value of negotiation as a very
               powerful tool for the settlement of disputes.

MALCOLM   I don't think we'd have won if the ladies hadn't
               joined in.

THOMO   What are you talking about . . . course we
               would! I were just toying with 'em.

NIGEL   No . . . credit where it's due, Thomo. I mean,
               you had rather lost your impact after they'd
               suspended you from the coat hooks. Is your
               stomach any better now?

THOMO | Now that 'as nothing to do wi' t' fight. I was all right. It was only later that I started feeling badly.

SHIRLEY | But you are feeling better now?

THOMO | Not entirely, no.

SHIRLEY | I thought you were a very brave soldier. Here, let me do your eye, love.

(SHIRLEY *moves to* THOMO *and gently holds the ice pack against his cheek, stroking his head with her other hand.* NIGEL *and* MALCOLM *watch jealously.*)

MALCOLM | (*looking hopefully at* LORRAINE) My head still throbs a bit.

LORRAINE | Does it? Oh . . . all right. 'Ere, let me soothe it for you.

MALCOLM | (*shyly*) Thank you.

(LORRAINE *moves to* MALCOLM *and gently massages the back of his neck.*)

NIGEL | (*hopefully*) And my shoulder's terribly painful.

KAY | I'll give you a couple of paracetamol when we get back to the hotel.

NIGEL | Thank you my love.

KAY | You're welcome.

(KAY *moves to the buffet table to nibble at some crisps.* SHIRLEY *and* LORRAINE *continue their ministrations.* JENNY *draws* MUGSY *to one side.*)

JENNY | I think I know what's wrong wi' Thomo's stomach. I think it's our fault.

MUGSY	Too much beer I bet. Thomo always used to drink too much beer. He were always throwing up all over t' place.
JENNY	No, it's the sausage rolls you made. Except they're not exactly what you could call *sausage* rolls!
MUGSY	'Ow do you mean.
JENNY	When I were in t' freezer getting some more ice out for 'is eye. All t' sausage meat's still in there.
MUGSY	But it can't be.
JENNY	What *is* missing is that minced pigs offal we got for t' cats. I told you there was something wrong wi' those sausage rolls . . . and Thomo's eaten most of 'em.
MUGSY	You mean Thomo's eaten all that . . . 'ey, magic . . . that's a laugh that isn't it! 'Ey, Thomo . . . you know all those sausage rolls you ate.
THOMO	Aye.
JENNY	(*elbowing* MUGSY *in the stomach to keep him quiet*) We hope you really enjoyed 'em don't we, Mugsy.
MUGSY	Oh, aye, yeah.
THOMO	Yes, I did thank you.
MUGSY	Magic. 'Ey, you didn't think they were offal did you . . . you know . . . awful . . . offal . . . do you get it?
THOMO	'Ow do you mean?
MUGSY	Oh, nowt. Magic . . . oink oink. I'll put a bit o' music on then shall I?

THOMO	There's no need.
MUGSY	No, it's no trouble.
	(MUGSY *moves up to his disco console.*)
NIGEL	(*rubbing his shoulder and groaning*) I don't think I'll be able to drive tomorrow, Kay.
KAY	Good, I'll drive . . . we may get back home in under ten hours!
NIGEL	(*groaning again*) Thing is . . . I think it's aggravated that old grouting injury.
	(NIGEL *looks glum.* KAY *notices his expression and relents. She moves to him and starts to massage his shoulder.*)
KAY	Come here you big soft thing.
NIGEL	Thank you.
KAY	But I don't want you getting any ideas for later.
NIGEL	No my love.
THOMO	'Ey, I think we showed 'em though didn't we . . . those 'ooligans.
NIGEL	Yes, I think we can say that tonight has been a great success. Particularly involving as it did the eventual turn-out of four patrol cars, three police dogs, a transit van, a paramedic and two ambulances.
MALCOLM	Not to mention the mounted policeman . . .
THOMO	And the 'elicopter.
NIGEL	Not a bad turn out that.

THOMO   Better than we used to manage in t' old days.
               We were lucky then if we could manage to get
               t' local bobby out on 'is push bike.

MALCOLM   Even I quite enjoyed it. It made the Co-op seem
               quite conservative by comparison. My trainee
               delicatessen assistant won't believe it when I
               tell him.

THOMO   Aye, well I've told you before, son, there's
               more to life than slicing corned beef.

NIGEL   Yes, all in all, a very satisfactory evening I
               think. A pity the others couldn't make it
               though.

THOMO   Aye, still, we were the *real* mates weren't we?
               The four of us. We were the nub.

NIGEL   I suppose we were, yes . . . I'd like to think so
               anyway. Perhaps you should revise your
               opinions, Malcolm. I don't think anybody who
               was involved in tonight's excitement could
               ever consider themselves to be insignificant
               . . . and I even include the ladies in that one.

MUGSY   (*moving forward*) It's funny, but I were just
               thinking about that.

THOMO   Oh, 'ere we go again! That bottle on the back
               of 'is 'ead 'as stimulated the small particle o'
               brain embedded in 'is skull.

MUGSY   No . . . it's dead important. You should think
               more o' yourself, Mal. We can't all be dead
               clever or dead important can we? But it's what
               goes on inside that matters . . . as long as we
               try to lead big lives.

NIGEL   A very noble sentiment, Mugsy.

MUGSY   It'd be crap if you got real old and then just sat
               there thinking you'd made a mess of
               everything. 'Specially when you think about

people like Jacko . . . 'e didn't 'ave a chance to
get old did 'e? We were 'is mates so it's up to
us to live life for 'im isn't it? We shouldn't
waste what we've got . . . even if it isn't very
much.

THOMO   Nice one, son. Aye, very nice that . . . almost
'ad the air of a poet about you for a minute
then, Mugs.

MALCOLM I think Jacko would have approved of tonight.
A night out with his mates . . . with all of *us*.

MUGSY   It's daft 'ow things turn out. That bloke I killed
wi' me bayonet . . . 'e was only a kid really. I
sometimes think that if things 'ad been
different . . . like he'd been born in t' next
street . . . e' might 'ave been a mate. Instead o'
that . . .

JENNY   (*putting her arm around him*) Don't, Mugsy
. . . it's all right.

MUGSY   I know. It's crap really but at least I 'ave got
mates . . . and I 'ave got you 'aven't I?

JENNY   Course you 'ave.

THOMO   And more to the point, Mugs, you 'ave got
three pubs. Now I've been thinking about that
and I was wondering if you did a bit o'
discount for mates . . . you know, if I were a
regular.

MUGSY   (*uncertain*) Yeah . . . course.

JENNY   (*warning*) Mugsy!

MUGSY   No, I can't really, Thomo . . . 'cos it's, like, me
job.

THOMO   I'd see you right . . . when you needed a motor
vehicle.

MUGSY	I can't drive. I'll tell you what . . . I'll stand t' cost of t' buffet tonight. (*To* JENNY.) That's all right isn't it?
JENNY	Yeah . . . if that's what you want. Shall I put some music on now? It's only 'alf past one, t' night's still young.
MUGSY	Yeah, magic.
	(JENNY *moves up to the platform.*)
THOMO	That just leaves one formality then.
	(THOMO *moves to pick up a lavatory brush which he has concealed in the room.*)
	We 'ave an initiation ceremony to perform. I 'ave the brush . . . all we need now is the pickled egg . . . you do still sell 'em I assume?
MUGSY	I've got one on t' table ready.
THOMO	That's very 'andy, Mugs. Unlike the victim to be so co-operative.
NIGEL	Ah, thing is . . . as it happens, Thomo, we had a chat while you were being treated in casualty.
THOMO	Yeah?
MALCOLM	It dawned on us. Because you always performed the initiation, you never actually went through it yourself.
THOMO	(*suddenly worried*) Of course not, no . . . but that doesn't matter . . . I mean, I were in charge. I were the Master of Ceremonies.
MALCOLM	We've decided that it does matter. We're going to do *you*.
KAY	That sounds exciting, can I help?

LORRAINE	I will as well.
NIGEL	Oh no, definitely not. It's not a pleasant sight. Anyway, only those in the know are allowed to participate.
KAY	But we are in the know, aren't we Lorraine?

(KAY *and* LORRAINE *join their right hands and go through the secret handshake routine performed by the men earlier.*)

KAY } LORRAINE	(*together*) Oggle, oggle, oggle . . . eek, eek, eek.
NIGEL	(*indignant*) How do you know that?
KAY	Sorry, Nigel . . . I peeked. Don't worry, your secret's safe with us.
NIGEL	I suppose you'd better help then. Would you like to grab hold of him, Mugsy?

(MUGSY *tries to grab* THOMO *who dodges out of the way.*)

THOMO	No you can't do this . . . not to me . . . not with ladies present!
MALCOLM	Yes we can.
THOMO	Tell 'em, Shirley.
SHIRLEY	Sorry, love, I think I'd better help Jenny.

(SHIRLEY *moves onto the platform with* JENNY.)

THOMO	No . . . it's not right. I'm not a well man, you know.
NIGEL	Neither are we.

(THOMO *backs away towards the door.* MUGSY,
NIGEL *and* MALCOLM *edge towards him.*)

THOMO   (*desperate*) We can talk about this lads . . . I
                 mean let's be reasonable. I'll tell you what . . .
                 we'll do a deal . . . we don't use the pickled
                 egg.

MUGSY   We don't want to miss 'owt. It wouldn't be
                 right.

THOMO   Well, no lavatory brush then . . .

                 (*They edge closer to him.*)

                 Oh . . . bloody 'ell.

                 (THOMO *runs out of the door, pursued by*
                 MUGSY, NIGEL *and* MALCOLM.)

KAY   (*sitting*) I think this is going to turn in to a
                 very long night! I think I'm rather enjoying it.

LORRAINE   (*sitting next to her*) And I 'aven't even started
                 on Mal yet!

                 (*The music starts to play as the lights fade and
                 the curtain falls. The end.*)

FURNITURE AND PROPERTY LIST

ACT ONE

Set
Platform with disco console, headphones and assorted records and CDs, with amateurish sign saying "Rockin Eddie's Mega Disco" fixed to console. Trestle table with buffet items covered by white cloth. Two or three pub tables with accompanying chairs.

During Cue 1:
(Page 14) Set empty and partially full glasses and bottles on tables.

During Cue 3:
(Page 49) Set nearly empty plates and drinks for NIGEL, THOMO and MUGSY.

Personal
Handbag (KAY)
Business card, dog-eared letter (THOMO)
Handbag (LORRAINE)

Offstage
Electrical leads (MUGSY)
Tray with 3 full pints and a half pint of beer (MALCOLM)
Tray with 3 drinks (LORRAINE)

ACT TWO

Set
Rearrange glasses, plates and bottles. Hidden lavatory brush.

Personal
Wad of paper notes (NIGEL)
Handbag containing wad of paper notes (KAY)

Offstage
Ice wrapped in a cloth (JENNY)
Sling (NIGEL)
Bar towel (MUGSY)
Plaster (THOMO)
Full pint of beer, head bandage (MALCOLM)

LIGHTING AND EFFECTS PLOT

All lighting is the interior of a room in a pub.

Cue 1   (Page 14) THOMO: ". . . get the bloody drinks in!"
         'Adam and the Ants' song starts playing.
         Lights fade.
         Music fades.
         Different music rises.
         Lights rise

Cue 2   (Page 48) JENNY: ". . . Here, try this one. It's one of
         his latest."
         Loud, fast song starts playing.

Cue 3   (Page 49) KAY *holds her head in her hands*.
         Lights fade.
         Music fades.
         Lights rise.

Cue 4   (Page 57) MUGSY: ". . . Just like old times really.
         Magic."
         Loud rock music starts playing.
         Lights fade.

Cue 5   (Page 62) MUGSY: ". . . 'Ey, do you remember this
         one?"
         Music plays.
         Lights fade.
         Lights rise stage right.

Cue 6   (Page 63) NIGEL: ". . . I'm not waiting any longer."
         Cross-fade lights from men, right to women, left.

Cue 7   (Page 64) KAY: ". . . I think you'd find microbiol-
         ogy a rather refreshing alternative, Lorraine."
         Cross-fade lights from women, left to men, right.

Cue 8   (Page 65) NIGEL: ". . . Now I have here a little aide
         memoire . . ."
         Cross-fade lights from men, right to women, left.

Cue 9	(Page 65) KAY: ". . . It took him weeks to research it . . . he's been an absolute pain." Cross-fade lights from women, left to men, right.
Cue 10	(Page 68) THOMO: "I thought we were talking about events, not catastrophes." Lights rise on women, left.
Cue 11	(Page 69) KAY: "See what I mean! It's a complete and utter waste of time." Lights fade on women, left.
Cue 12	(Page 70) THOMO: ". . . I've 'ad to raise a family on my mental whatsname . . . support a wife and kids." Cross-fade lights from men, right to women, left.
Cue 13	(Page 71) SHIRLEY: ". . . and I ruined that by expecting so much more." Cross-fade lights from women, left to men, right.
Cue 14	(Page 72) THOMO: "I'm warning you, son." Cross-fade lights from men, right to women, left.
Cue 15	(Page 72) SHIRLEY: ". . . it was just a chance to cheer each other up." Cross-fade lights from women, left to men, right.
Cue 16	(Page 75) NIGEL: ". . . or an Obama, but hardly what I would call a small life." Cross-fade lights from men, right to women, left.
Cue 17	(Page 76) JENNY: ". . . And a PhD in Digital Communication and Data Transfer Systems. Cheers." Cross-fade lights from women, left to men, right.
Cue 18	(Page 80) MUGSY: ". . . Not when they saw what I'd done." Cross-fade lights from men, right to women, left.

Cue 19   (Page 80) JENNY: ". . . He doesn't just work 'ere, he owns it ... this and another two of 'em."
Lights rise on men, right.

Cue 20   (Page 80) THOMO: "Bloody 'ell!"
Light fade.
Music plays.
Lights rise.
(After several seconds) Music fades.

Cue 21   (Page 92) SHIRLEY: ". . . It's not too late to get the police."
Sound of commotion, off. Shouting and crashing noises.

Cue 22   (Page 92) SHIRLEY: "You don't believe everything he says do you?"
Sound of commotion off, culminating in a loud crashing noise.

Cue 23   (Page 94) KAY: "Aren't they all, Shirley, aren't they all."
Sound of extended commotion off . As noise fades a bottle is thrown past the door in the corridor.

Cue 24   (Page 94) NIGEL: "Now just you stop that right now . . .".
A bottle is thrown over NIGEL'S head as he ducks in the corridor.

Cue 25   (Page 95) NIGEL: "Oh! Jolly good."
NIGEL steps out of doorway and ducks just before a bottle passes over his head.

Cue 26   (Page 95) NIGEL: ". . . I said stop that. You're not listening to me are you."
Sound of commotion, off.

Cue 27   (Page 96) MUGSY: ". . . It's magic is this."
          Sound of gradually noisier and extended commo-
          tion, off.

Cue 28   (Page 97) SHIRLEY exits, carrying a trifle.
          Music plays.
          Lights fade.
          Music fades
          Lights rise.

Cue 29   (Page 106) LORRAINE: "And I 'aven't even started
          on Mal yet!"
          Music plays.
          Lights fade.

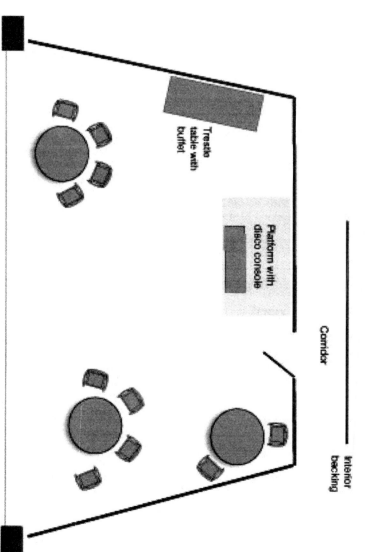

Trestle table with buffet

Platform with disco console

Corridor

Interior backing